ARI'EL INSTITUT

ARI'EL INSTITUTE

INTERNATIONAL JOURNAL OF BIBLICAL STUDIES

ISSUE 10

ARI'EL INSTITUTE

Ari'el International Ministries and the Ari'el Institute group are the missions' arm and the ministerial development group for the international and extended work of the Gospel Assembly Church of Mansfield, Ohio.

The Ari'el Institute International Journal is published quarterly for the benefit of those ministers and other Bible students who are part of this ministry.

ARI'EL INSTITUTE

MINISTERIAL NOTE

The following ministerial comments are included in each edition of this journal in order to clarify its purpose and content.

The impetus for compiling these journals was the result of requests by our extended ministry and saints (particularly outside of the United States) for printed materials for study. As such, the material here is primarily intended for the use of the ministers and saints who are part of our extended work. For that reason, we hope that any outside of our work who may receive these materials understand that their intent is not to address issues in a general ministerial sense, or to present teaching to the Body as a whole, but as a tool to communicate our teachings to those we are responsible for.

Studies and notes from ministerial discussions that are included here are <u>not</u> intended to be taken as an official expression of the general teaching of the Body of Christ, since all of these interpretive viewpoints are not settled or set in stone. For this reason, ideas and interpretations presented here are not to be taken as dogmatic statements or inflexible declarations. We strongly believe in the progressive revelation of truth and of the restoration of the church. Both of these beliefs color our conception of biblical discussion and demand the realization that there is still greater and clearer truth yet to be known. No claim is made by our ministry to origination of truth or of possession of a final, finished, fully developed doctrinal package of beliefs. We are still striving for the fullness of the faith that was once delivered to the saints, and the material presented here is only an expression of that act of striving, not a completed or comprehensive work.

This kind of printed format allows us several benefits that we believe justify its use. First, it provides a vehicle for study and discussion among our new brethren and churches that is easier to follow than only listening to sermons and Bible studies in an audio format. Second, printed material can allow for a fuller consideration of a topic and a simpler study process.

There are two other significant reasons that this format is effective for us. First, shipping of materials overseas can be very cost prohibitive, especially when a large number of shipments are required. Second, many of the churches and brethren we are working with overseas are in areas where internet access is limited or very costly. This makes it difficult for them to listen to online audio or download multimedia materials. This format helps to address these last two challenges. For those who do receive physical materials, a compilation of this kind lessens our shipping load. For those who are able to go online, downloading this journal in PDF format allows for quick and easy access.

As to the overall content, this will include study articles on different passages in the Bible, topical studies, word studies, short messages, and other material intended for the use of the brethren and saints we are directly working with. We may also periodically put together "special editions" entirely dedicated to a single key topic that is critical to our foundational teaching. The bulk of each issue consists of a transcription of the ongoing discussion occurring in the Ari'el Institute online group: a members only, private social media group that allows interaction and discussion in a completely closed and non-public atmosphere. This includes a selection of the questions and comments received in that group and the responses and discussion each instigates.

This material is principally technical and theological in nature rather than pastoral (Christian living, marriage, family life, children, and similar subjects). Pastoral discussion on these subjects will be periodically included, but most pastoral subjects are included in our quarterly church newsletter where practical subjects related to home life and church work are discussed, and meeting reports and other materials are provided. Discussion among the ministry that are part of the Ari'el International group on pastoral subjects tend to be in a confidential and closed personal setting rather than in the type of open discussions included in these journals This particular format is intended to address doctrinal and biblical issues, which are foundational to our identity as a Body of churches, which set us apart from mainstream Christendom and deeper subjects still in a developmental stage.

Any thoughts or input on upcoming issues are warmly and humbly appreciated.

Bro. Daniel Baer

Gospel Assembly Church of Mansfield, Ohio
Ari'el International

IS THERE SPIRITUAL AND PRACTICAL VALUE IN STUDYING THE LANGUAGES OF THE BIBLE OR, AT LEAST, IN LOOKING AT THE MEANING OF THE HEBREW, ARAMAIC, AND GREEK WORDS THAT THE BIBLE WAS WRITTEN IN?

BRO. DANIEL BAER

I strongly believe (based on many evidences) that the languages of the Bible that underlie translations (English or otherwise) should be examined when we are studying the Scripture, especially when making a deep analysis of a passage or statement. Studying (or at least looking at) the original language of the Bible can be powerfully effective in getting a deeper spiritual understanding of what passages and words may be conveying and in learning some rich practical lessons as well.

The following examples of several Greek words in the New Testament are stark evidence of this. Knowing what these Greek words express in their deepest root meaning teaches a beautiful lesson that is not obvious in the English translation of these words. This is not only interesting or even inspiring to know, it makes the meaning of passages come to life in a far more potent way than is present in the surface-level text of the English. Knowing the meaning of the Hebrew and Greek words can tell us something about what God really intended to express when He chose the words that He did. These words are not always synonymous in meaning with the words they are translated into in other languages, and they can unquestionably carry a much deeper and broader meaning in the original languages than that conveyed by other languages. Some words are too complex in meaning to be perfectly and fully conveyed by just one word in another language when it is being translated. That is very easy to see if you study the original languages. Sometimes the meaning of a word in Greek simply cannot be encapsulated in one single word in English. The idea being conveyed by the Greek word is simply not communicated completely by any one English word. Thus, the best translators can do is to choose a word that conveys a similar meaning.

So, if the original languages that God chose to write the Bible in had words with root meanings that are more detailed and deeper than the words they were translated into (and they absolutely do), or if the meaning of some of the original words is more complex than any single word in another language that it might be translated into, that alone is sufficient reason to study those languages or examine their basic meaning when studying the Bible.

I have known individuals who were resistant to any inclusion of the meaning of the original languages in biblical discussion state that all we need is the English words of the *King James Version* alone (along with the Spirit's illumination of course), and that there is no need to ever look at any other references in order to understand its words and message. There are some very simple reasons why that is not the case and why even those who are most adamant about not needing to look at the meaning of the original language are almost certainly contradicting themselves with their claims. There are many words in English translations (the *King James Version* especially) of which the meaning may not be correctly or fully understood by readers, and in some cases readers may not know what the word means at all, despite being native English speakers. This could be due to words in a translation being in archaic forms or expressions, or words that were chosen by the translators being vocabulary words that are not understood by the average reader. What do you do if you do not know the meaning of the words in the *King James Version*? Does the *King James Version* alone (without studying anything else, including an English dictionary) define every word the translators chose? Of course not.

Perhaps the vocabulary used in the *King James Version* includes a word that a reader doesn't understand (in terms of its meaning or use). "Dissimulation" is an example of this. It is a word many English speakers may not know the meaning of, and I have heard some completely misdefine and misuse it because they never bothered to look it up in a dictionary since they thought they could define it by the context of the passage it was in. That is not always possible. What does a reader have to do when they come across the word "dissimulation" if they do not know its meaning? Is simply reading the *King James Version* (without going outside of it to study the definition of the word) going to give them the full meaning of that word? Of course not. They will have to look it up in an English dictionary which, by the way, may have a range of definitions that they will then have to analyze to determine which is the correct one. Added to this is the fact that the word in English may not precisely or fully express what the original Greek word meant.

So, if there are words a reader of a translation does not understand, he will certainly have to go to another source outside his English translation to define what they mean. Isn't that exactly what we are doing when we look at the Greek meaning of the word? But, doing so is better; we are not just looking at the possible range of meanings the English word it was translated into might have, we are looking at the meaning of the original word that the English word was translated from. Thus, it is impossible to argue that it is not necessary (or at least wise) to look at (and potentially study out) the original language of the Bible. Doing so is no different (though more accurate) than going to an English dictionary to figure out what a word in your English translation means.

The same thing is true for a number of other similar issues in the English translations. Perhaps the vocabulary the *King James Version* uses is a word that has changed in meaning in the more than 400 years since that translation was made. There are many examples of such words in the *King James Version*, such as the word "letteth" in **2 Thessalonians 2:7**, which now means "to allow", but in the jargon of the period that translation was made in meant "to prevent". That meaning is the exact opposite of that which a modern English-speaking reader would take from that word. For most people, the language of the *King James Version* in **2 Thessalonians 2:7** (and in numerous other places) will not be properly understood without other reference material that explains that "letteth" does not mean what most reading it today would think it does. So, do we (or at least most people) need additional linguistic reference material to properly understand words in the earlier English translations that have changed in meaning? Certainly. Once again, how is this any different than studying the meaning of the original language? We are simply studying the meaning of the original words, as originally understood, to examine whether they may have a different meaning than is conveyed by the language in the translation we are using. If we didn't understand the meaning of an archaic or difficult English word in an English translation, we would have to look to a reference work on English to determine its meaning. Wouldn't it be more reasonable to look at the actual original word's meaning rather than just the meaning of a word that it was translated into, in some cases, more than 1500 years after the original was written?

There are many other examples of these kinds of issues that must be considered, and they demonstrate why, no matter how great a translation may be, we do need to study below and behind the surface text of the translations we use in order to properly and fully understand what they are saying, and if the words the translators chose are not affected by doctrinal or personal bias.

As to the deeper, richer meanings of some of the words in the original languages, the words the Spirit inspired Paul to choose in **1 Corinthians 13:7** contains a beautiful example.

1 Corinthians 13:7 (Charity*) Beareth all things, believeth all things, hopeth all things, endureth all things.*

The words translated "beareth" and "endureth" are very near synonyms of one another and often can have overlapping meanings in English. Trying to determine what "beareth" might mean in parallel or in contrast to "endureth" would require a person to study both in an English dictionary and then to determine what meanings (of several) might be meant by them. Some might conclude that they are just repetitions of one another, especially if they compare them with the other two words in this statement ("believeth" and "hopeth"), which are also very similar in meaning.

But, when the Greek words that these English words were translated from are examined in detail, a rich tapestry of deeper meaning is revealed that teaches a key lesson on what kind of "bearing" and "enduring" this is meant to express.

The Greek word *stego*, translated "beareth", literally (in its root meaning) means "to cover" something (like a blanket covering something or a roof covering a house).

The Greek word *hypomeno*, translated "endureth", literally (in its root meaning) means "to bear up from beneath" or "to stay beneath (or under)" something.

Not only will you not see those meanings by just reading the English, you will not see them by looking them up in an English dictionary. In fact, the meaning of the word "bear" in an English dictionary would be more similar to the other Greek word in this verse that is translated "endure". And, those meanings are rich and deep and contain powerful, practical lessons we need to learn as Christians. I imagine a potent message could be preached on each of those words alone just based on their underlying root meanings. Added to this is the fact that, in English, to "bear" something usually refers to carrying it or being under its weight, which is what the other word in the passage is talking about and *not* what this word is expressing, as it is almost the opposite in meaning.

Knowing the meaning of the Greek words in **1 Corinthians 13:7** tells us several theological and practical things. One of them is that our "bearing" with others requires us to "cover" some things with charity.

Proverbs 10:12 *Hatred stirreth up strifes: but love covereth all sins.*

Someone reading the word "beareth" in the *King James Version* may get a good lesson from its meaning, but they would not get the full intent of the original word it was translated from.

As to "enduring", how poignant that word becomes when we understand that it is referring to bearing up under weight or being under pressure. Not just "enduring" in a general sense, but specifically enduring a load of pressure and weight that you are under. Once again, knowing what the word "enduring" means in English will not convey this deeper point which, I am absolutely certain (just as with the rest of the words in this verse), *was* intended to be understood in its full meaning.

Will every reader of the Bible be able to simply pick up the Bible and see this in their English translation alone? Of course not. But, every reader will not be able to understand the correct meaning of a number of words and statements in an English translation if they do not look them up in a dictionary, so why would we not look them up in the language they were originally written in which includes many words having deeper and more precise meanings than can be conveyed in the languages they might be translated into?

One other example is the Greek word *diakonos* sometimes translated "deacon" in the Bible. "Deacon" is a word some English speakers may misunderstand or even misapply in its meaning as it has been used in the English. This word is an important example for several reasons: First, in the English language there have been a multiplicity of meanings given to it. That means that simply looking at its English definitions (and how different churches have defined it as well) may not be helpful at all, especially if you apply the wrong meaning. Second, added to that is the fact that it is not always translated in the *King James Version* in the same way (as is the case with many words in that and other English translations) which may lead readers to misunderstand what it is referring to if they do not look at the underlying Greek word.

Diakonos was translated in at least three ***different*** ways in the *King James Version*. It was translated as some form of the word "minister" about twenty times, as some form of the word "servant" about eight times, and as the word "deacons" three times.

Someone only reading the English translation of the *King James Version*, without looking at the Greek from which it was translated, might incorrectly conclude that these are three different words when they are actually only one word. A reader might make the mistake of differentiating between the words "minister" and "deacon" in the passages when both are actually the same Greek word *diakonos*, and thus confuse the two in those contexts.

Diakonos is far broader in scope than the way the English words "deacon" and "minister" are used and, when its underlying meaning is understood, far richer in its theological texture. ***Diakonos*** simply refers to someone who "ministers" to the needs of others. That is why it could mean a "servant", "minister", etc. But, its meaning is much deeper than just "one who ministers" or "one who serves". Knowing its root meaning in the Greek not only tells us that it refers to someone who "ministers" but to how they do so. The root from which the Greek word ***diakonos*** comes from literally means, "under rower". It comes from the idea of the work of a rower on a Greek trireme or other type of ship with oars, especially those kinds of ships which had the rowers down ***under*** the deck rowing. Often in the ancient world, these were slaves chained to the oars that they were pulling. This paints a stark and humbling portrait of the kind of work of the ministry that this word is expressing. One who is carrying out the role of a ***diakonos*** may be said to be doing so ***below the deck***. This is a servant of the ship who is rowing so that it can keep moving forward. This is one who has been ***chained to the oar***, completely committed to his responsibility. This is one who is not presently ***on the deck***, in the spotlight, but who is working behind the scenes doing the difficult, menial, and sometimes thankless work that is not often noticed or appreciated, but which is critical for forward momentum.

This dramatic, poetic imagery is not as present in the English words "servant", "minister", or "deacon", as none of those words have the underlying root meaning that ***diakonos*** does. Someone reading or studying the Greek might see that meaning and get a far deeper and more layered message from the text than someone could by simply reading the words "servant", "minister", or "deacon" in the English. There is a very important lesson in the root meaning of ***diakonos*** that all who desire to be leaders (and proper servants as well) should learn. Those who want to serve the "ship" (the church), whether as leaders or laboring laity, must be willing to toil "under the deck" at times (and often for some time before they are ready to work "on the deck"), working out of the spotlight where, very often, the labor is hard and many may not even see them doing it.

No matter what role ministers may eventually hold (perhaps rising to a place in God where he is leading from the "deck of ship"), all should begin in spirit and in practice as "under rowers": working in a place of service and ministry that may not be as visible, as likely to garner credit, or to receive attention and approbation. That is the most common course of the calling and commissioning of a minister of God. He will always be a "servant", and he must be willing to serve in any capacity. Particularly in the developmental stages of his ministerial labor (normally under another minister or overseer). A man must be willing to work outside of the spotlight and the limelight. He must be willing to labor in the most difficult and even mundane places of service, as it is very often his willingness to work "under the deck", quietly laboring with all his strength to move the church forward – that will be the beginning of him making full proof of his call to the ministry, and which will purchase to him a good degree.

2 Timothy 4:5 *But watch thou in all things, endure afflictions, do the work of an evangelist, make full proof of thy ministry* (the noun form ***diakonia***).

1 Timothy 3:13 *For they that have used the office of a deacon* (the verb form ***diakaneo***) *well purchase to themselves a good degree, and great boldness in the faith which is in Christ Jesus.*

The point of the preceding examples is that there are deeper, richer, and fuller meanings of the message of the Scripture which is possible to be seen only when the original languages it was written in are, at the very least, examined. And, the more they are studied, the richer the layers of their meaning.

That knowledge is not necessary to understand foundational salvation truths since they are clearly conveyed in the translations. But, that knowledge will greatly enhance a person's understanding of many biblical subjects and concepts, and in some cases will clarify and correct their misconceptions regarding the meaning of the text.

WHY WE DO NEED TO STUDY THE MEANING OF THE ORIGINAL LANGUAGES OF THE BIBLE

IF A READER DOES NOT UNDERSTAND THE MEANING OF ONE OF THE FOLLOWING WORDS FOUND IN THE NEW TESTAMENT IN THE *KING JAMES VERSION* (AND SOME OTHER ENGLISH TRANSLATIONS), HOW CAN HE PROPERLY DEFINE THEM?

"DEACON"

Problem: this word has been defined in a variety of different ways in the English language

How do we know which is the right meaning?

How does a reader of an English translation determine what the word "deacon" refers to if they cannot do so simply and entirely by context (which cannot be done)?

LOOK AT THE MEANING OF THE "ENGLISH" WORD IN AN ENGLISH DICTIONARY?

Which of the multiple meanings and ways this word has been used in English is what God meant when He inspired the original Greek word *diakonos* ("deacon") to be written?

If several different possible meanings of this English word could fit into the context of the passages where it is found, how can we determine which is actually meant?

Is the English word "deacon" even English in origin? NO, it is Latin. *Diacon* (deacon) is a Latin word taken directly from the Greek *diakonos* (thus, it wasn't an English word to begin with, but the Greek word used in the Bible)

"DISSIMULATION"

Problem: this word is a technical term that is archaic in its language and almost entirely unfamiliar in meaning to modern English readers

How does a reader of an English translation determine what the word "dissimulation" means if they cannot do so simply and entirely by context (which cannot be done)?

LOOK AT THE MEANING OF AN "ENGLISH" WORD IN AN ENGLISH DICTIONARY?

Which of the multiple possible meanings and ways this word has been used in English is what God meant when He inspired the original Greek word *anypokritos* ("dissimulation") to be written?

If several different possible meanings of this English word could fit into the context of the passages where it is found, how can we determine which is actually meant?

Is the English word "dissimulation" even English in origin? NO, it is Latin. *Dissimulation* is the Latin stem of *dissimulatio*

How is doing so any different or any better in trying to determine the meaning of these words than simply looking in a Greek lexicon or dictionary to begin with?

LOOK AT THE MEANING OF THE ACTUAL, ORIGINAL GREEK WORDS OF THE NEW TESTAMENT

This does ***not*** require any advanced education, as anyone capable of reading can look at a dictionary or lexicon of the Greek (Strong's, etc.), and read the definition just as simply as doing so for an English word in an English dictionary, but instead of reading the definition of a word used to interpret a Greek word, they will be reading the definition of the actual, original word written by the writers of the Scripture as the Spirit moved upon them. And, the very poorly considered argument that there is no point in looking at or studying the original words of the original Scripture because they can have multiple meanings is inept for several reasons. First, there are many words in the original languages that do ***not*** have multiple meanings, or if they do have multiple meanings, the only possible meaning is easily determined by the context and grammar of the passage they are found in . Second, how is that any different from English? English words have the very same problem of having potential multiple meanings, so that argument is nullified by the fact that the same is true of the English. If we may have to look up and study the meaning of English words in order to understand an English translation of the original Greek New Testament, why wouldn't we just look up and study the meaning of the Greek words to begin with?

ARI'EL INSTITUTE GROUP DISCUSSION NOTES

The following is a portion of the ongoing discussions in the Ari'el Institute group online as well as questions sent to our ministry. This principally includes questions and input from ministers and saints that are part of our international work. There is also input from those who are part of the general Body here in the United States and new ministers from various backgrounds who are reaching out to our ministry both here and abroad. In the latter cases, those interacting who are new ministers from other backgrounds are sometimes noted as to their denominational background. This is intended to help clarify their potential interpretive positions.

For the sake of the anonymity of the international ministry, many of whom are in areas where there is great political and religious persecution, all names are shortened to initials. The same initials may often be different individuals. In addition, very often one individual who may be asking questions or interacting may doing so in a representative capacity for a group of other ministers they themselves are responsible for. Bro. Baer's name is spelled out because he is often addressing questions or acting in the capacity of moderator for the group.

Discussions are arranged by the key subjects they address and in the general order in which they occurred at the time. Each issue will contain discussions that occurred approximately a year prior to its publication. In some cases, a subject is addressed in one discussion that continued in later discussions. In those cases, they are included together with a line break between them to clarify this. Some of the topics and questions addressed will be covered in greater detail in upcoming issues.

Questions and comments are unedited and left in the original format in which they were expressed (capitalization, italics, etc.), other than when very light editing was necessary due to language barriers which may have not made statements understandable. Words may also be added as "filler" in unique cases where the original statement was uncertain. There are also a number of cases in which comments were abbreviated due to statements made that were unrelated to the discussion though most statements of feedback have been included.

ARI'EL INSTITUTE

Bro. Baer asked that we also note that his approach in these types of discussions is intentionally less dogmatic than might be the case in the local church. His intent has been to present and address various views, including those that are presently only theoretical in nature.

Jude 3
*...earnestly contend for the faith
which was once delivered unto the saints.*

Philippians 1:27
*...stand fast in one spirit,
with one mind striving together for the faith of the gospel;*

THE "STARS" IN JOB 38:7

BRO. D.C.: What are some thoughts on the following verses?

Job 38:4, 7 *Where wast thou when I laid the foundations of the earth? declare, if thou hast understanding. ... When the morning stars sang together, and all the sons of God shouted for joy?*

BRO. D.D.P.: God is simply using examples to show Job how little he knows and understands compared to what God knows and understands Brother C.

BRO. D.C.: Yes sir, but the wording has me curious about the difference between the stars and the sons of God. Is there any significance to the two?

BRO. D.D.P.: That depends on whether a person believes the "stars" and "sons of God" are human beings or celestial angels. Since I believe they are human beings, I don't see any significance to them other than God showing Job that God's understanding has existed from before the day of creation down through history until Job's time here on this earth.

BRO. J.P.: All of **Job 38** is symbolic and allegorical language describing the fall and redemption of man. To understand it, one must go to the beginning of the order of creation. The stars were created on the fourth day and the man on the sixth day, and in Luke the first man is called the son of God.

Luke 3:38 *...Adam, which was the son of God.*

So, we can say that the first son of God of the earthly creation was Adam, and the first in the spiritual creation was Jesus.

Who were these stars and children of God? According to the Bible, angels are not called children of God.

Hebrews 1:5 *For unto which of the angels said he at any time, Thou art my Son, this day have I begotten thee? And again, I will be to him a Father, and he shall be to me a Son?*

In **Job 1**, when it says Satan was among the children of God, those were not angels, but human children of God.

Job 1:6 *Now there was a day when the sons of God came to present themselves before the LORD, and Satan came also among them.*

So the children of God in Job 38:7 have to be of the new creation! As to the stars of the dawn, who are they? They are the first prophets and patriarchs in Genesis are called children of God.

Genesis 37:9-10 *And he dreamed yet another dream, and told it his brethren, and said, Behold, I have dreamed a dream more; and, behold, the sun and the moon and the eleven stars made obeisance to me. And he told it to his father, and to his brethren: and his father rebuked him, and said unto him, What is this dream that thou hast dreamed? Shall I and thy mother and thy brethren indeed come to bow down ourselves to thee to the earth?*

Then we can understand when they praised all the stars in Job 38:7.

Job 38:7 *When the morning stars sang together, and all the sons of God shouted for joy?*

This is just figurative language referring to the patriarchs and prophets who saw by the Spirit the new creation, in the redemption of the Messiah who saw coming.

Job 19:25-27 *For I know that my redeemer liveth, and that he shall stand at the latter day upon the earth: And though after my skin worms destroy this body, yet in my flesh shall I see God: Whom I shall see for myself, and mine eyes shall behold, and not another; though my reins be consumed within me.*

Hebrews 11:13 *These all died in faith, not having received the promises, but having seen them afar off, and were persuaded of them, and embraced them, and confessed that they were strangers and pilgrims on the earth.*

They looked at him from afar, believing it, and greeting him, and confessing, praised God for the new creation in Jesus Christ. Job knew this because he was a priest, like the father-in-law of Moses, the firstborn of his family according to the law of the firstborn had the obligation to make sacrifices for the sin of his family.

Job 1:5 *And it was so, when the days of their feasting were gone about, that Job sent and sanctified them, and rose up early in the morning, and offered burnt offerings according to the number of them all: for Job said, It may be that my sons have sinned, and cursed God in their hearts. Thus did Job continually.*

These were the children of God. Amen!

BRO. BAER: Brethren, I love allegory and symbolism as well. The problem with the preceding allegorical interpretation is that it does not match the actual biblical usage of these terms. Sometimes we can get so carried away with what looks like (to us) clear connections and snapping together of symbolic puzzle pieces that, put together seem to paint a certain picture, that we fail to look close enough at their details and just blend them together into a picture to support our presuppositions. When examined up close, with the rules of biblical consistency and context applied, the connections you are attempting to make simply cannot be made to fit. From a distance they look like they form a picture, but examined up close it becomes clear that the pieces and parts of the (supposed) picture have been forced together in unnatural and unbiblical ways (not in agreement with how the Bible actually does use this language). Based on your view of the nature of angels and of Satan in Job, you *need* to fit these pieces together (as otherwise you will have a serious challenge with explaining what is occurring in **Job 1** and **Job 2**). We cannot just force connections between what appear to be similar things in the Bible (improper application of allegorization) to try to force our ideas on or into the text (in this case the belief you hold that angels cannot be called "sons of God"). We have to not only look for possible connections, we have to properly define the things we are connecting in light of how the Bible uses them. In other words, you may want to avoid connecting "sons of God" and "morning stars" with celestial angels, but it is not what we want, or what we have already predetermined has to be so, it is what is: what is biblically true; what is how the Bible uses these terms. And, we cannot push and pry our presuppositions into the Scripture. Our interpretations must be biblically consistent in their defining of terms (how the Bible uses this language elsewhere, or even if it uses it in multiple ways: to refer to humans or celestial angels, for example) and contextual in our understanding of those terms (not reading something into or out of them that is not supported by the context of the passage they are found in).

The context of the reference to the "morning stars" and "sons of God" in **Job 38:7** (the verses that precede it and follow it) describes them as being present at the original creation when the *first* elements of the earth were being created. For that reason alone, it is not possible to claim they are human "sons of God". It is highly inappropriate to allegorize the meaning of those statements so heavily that their language is no longer even recognizable in meaning. We must not "spiritualize" away the most obvious and clear meaning of a passage simply because not doing so will contradict our beliefs. The context of **Job 38** has nothing to do with the patriarchs, their vision of a coming Messiah, or of the new creation. The entire context is that of God describing his creative power and power over creation. Not a future creation, but a past creation, which statement leads to another point. We must not obliviate the language and grammar of a passage by overwriting it with our own ideas. The language of **Job 38:7**, and that of the verses around it, is that of events that occurred in the past, and not events yet to occur in a new creation in the future. We don't get to allegorize away the language and grammar of a passage when it was God Himself who chose that language and grammar, which is doubly true in this passage. God not only inspired these words to be spoken by the Spirit, He was actually speaking them Himself!

Job 38:4-11 is one single poetic series of verses in the original Hebrew, all addressing one single set of events: the original creation. It is describing events that occurred ***before*** Adam was even created, so it would be contextually impossible (without using extreme allegorization and hyperbole) to make these "sons" and "stars" anything other than celestial angels. This is not only true because of the events that are being described, which could only be referring to the time of the creation prior to the creation of human beings (just consider what God is describing being created and established in this passage), it is also true because of the very grammar that God Himself chose to use. He refers to these events as having occurred in the past, before Job was even in existence, and not to events yet to occur in the future. We will avoid improper allegorization if we consider some of these things before we rush to make connections that cannot be made to fit together no matter how much they might appear so from a distance. Once we get close enough to the picture to look at the language, grammar, etc., it becomes clear that such connections simply cannot be made.

So, where does that leave us? If the context and the grammar of **Job 38** can only be referring to the past, and a past period prior to the human creation at that, then is there any biblical basis for referring to any celestial beings as "sons of God" or "morning stars?" The fact that human beings can be referred to as "sons of God" or "stars" (though perhaps not "morning stars") does not nullify those same titles being used for celestial beings as we will see. And, given that the context of **Job 38:7** cannot be referring to human beings (at least not if we don't force that interpretation on the text and the context and completely change the grammar to mean the exact opposite of what God actually did say), then is there a biblical basis for it referring to celestial beings?

This same kind of title of "morning star" is clearly used for at least one celestial being: Christ himself (**Revelation 22:16**). Brethren, this is why preconceptions bother me so much. We get a presuppositional belief in our mind about celestial angels and then overlay the clear and obvious meaning of passages with a heavy allegorical blanket to make it (supposedly) mean something that supports that presupposition. The reason some do not want to accept that this is referring to angels as "sons of God" (and this is not the only passage that does so if the original Hebrew is examined) is because referring to them in that way might contradict their presuppositions about celestial angels (and by extension might contradict their beliefs about one angel in particular). Ancient Jewish and Christian commentators *never* claimed that the individuals in **Job 38:7** were anything but celestial angels and the entire context supports that claim.

BRO. D.C.: Bro. Baer, thank you for your input. Would you mind explaining your take on verse seven? What is the scenario or event there, and what is the difference between the stars and sons? The reason this verse intrigued me is due to what Hebrews says about angels, that they were never called sons of God.

Hebrews 1:5 *For unto which of the angels said he at any time, Thou art my Son, this day have I begotten thee? And again, I will be to him a Father, and he shall be to me a Son?*

BRO. BAER: One of the common poetic forms found in the Hebrew language and literature is repetition of two things that are referred to in slightly different ways or with different titles that are actually the same thing that are referred to in two ways or with two titles poetically to give more than one side or perspective of what they are. I personally think the "morning stars" and "sons of God" here are one of two things: They are either two titles for the same group of angels or they are two categories of angels. If the latter were true, the title "morning stars" might refer to the highest class of celestial angelic beings (given that it is also used of Jesus). If so, then "sons of God" might be a more general reference to the whole angelic host. Thus, the highest celestial angels and the whole host of celestial angels. If the former were the case, it could be referring to morning stars, also called sons of God (which would be true of the latter regardless).

I think some of the statements in **Hebrews 1** that contrast Jesus with celestial angels is not making the point that angels cannot be called "sons of God", but that none of the angels were given the place of the unique and singular "Son of God". Though a number of beings (celestial or terrestrial) might be called "sons of God" in one way or another, there is only one being in this special place of sonship that Jesus holds as

"The Son of God". We are re-creations of the Spirit (Spirit-filled and born again) and are called "sons of God", though (just like the celestial angels who might be called "sons of God") none of us are the "Son of God" in the exact way that Jesus is. I believe that the title "son(s) of God" is referring to an individual who was created by the Spirit. All of the angels would have been created by the Spirit as was Jesus himself. If this were true then Adam himself *may* have been called a "son of God" when he was created, and this *might* be alluded to in Jesus' genealogy in **Luke 3**. Adam is referred to as "the son of God" in **Luke 3:38**, though the words "the son" are in italics which means that they are not present in the original Greek. I do think they may have been meant to be inferred as present though as in these types of genealogies the Jews often only used the full phrase "the son of" in the first statement of the genealogy (as is found here where only the first statement in the list actually says "Jesus... the son of Joseph". Every other "the son" is in italics (not actually part of the original) so these actually say "Joseph, which was of Heli", etc. The word "son" is intended to be inferred as part of each statement. The reason I bring all this up is that it is possible (as I just said) that only those who are direct creations by the Spirit (Jesus, celestial angels, and possibly Adam) or those who are re-creations by the Spirit (born again by Spirit baptism) are called sons of God in this kind of way in the Bible. Every human after Adam and Eve were the product of their human parents. They were not truly what could be thought of as direct creations of the Spirit. The only other examples in the Bible that (I personally believe) might refer to a "son of God" is in a more corporate way, such as when God referred to the nation of Israel as His son (singular). It wasn't that all the Israelites were directly Spirit created people (like those born again by the Spirit under the New Covenant), but that the nation itself was a product of God's Spirit (gathering the people together, keeping them together, protecting them, providing for them, directing them, giving them the Law, etc.).

Depending on how someone might interpret several other passages, the use of the title "sons of God" as a potential reference to celestial beings may only be used a handful of times in the Bible, but we have to be careful not to conclude that the number of times a title is used for one type of being (humans) obviates it being used for anyone or anything else. If we conclude that titles and words that are only used a couple of times for a certain person or thing in the Bible always and only refer to other persons or types of things that have the same title, we are going to force ourselves into some incorrect assumptions and biblical contradictions. For example, the title "king" is used far more for human kings than for Jesus, but that does not mean that even if it was only used once for him (it is used more than once of course), we would have to conclude that he was only human. There are times when someone is called something just one time in the entire Bible, and other people are called the same title or description many times, but we do not steal the one person's identity because others have the same title. We need to try to discover the whole range of how different titles are used. That issue feathers the edge of one of the most divisive doctrines among us though, so I will not develop it fully here.

Jesus is only directly called the "Lamb" a handful of times in only two books of the Bible, both of which are written by the same single person. The vast majority of times the titles "lamb" or "sheep" are used in the Bible (hundreds of times) they are referring to literal animals or to human beings in a figurative way. If we just took the many times the title "lamb" or "sheep" are used to refer to a human being and then claimed that Jesus being called the "Lamb" then means he was and is a human being (and never was a celestial being, or is not presently in a glorified state that is more than merely human), we would be making a grave mistake. Many humans are called "lambs" or "sheep", and Jesus is only called this in a bare handful of passages in comparison, but the many more examples of humans being called by these titles does not mean that the title as applied to Jesus identifies him as less than a celestial being. Without diving into this simple fact, that is what some unfortunately do with other titles in the Bible. They find examples of a title used for humans and then conclude (because of a predisposed doctrinal position that they hold) that the same title cannot be used for a celestial being. That is a bit unbiblical, given that celestial beings (like Jesus bearing the title "Lamb") can have the very same titles as human beings (like humans bearing the title "lambs" or "sheep"). In part this is because these human beings (called "lambs" or "sheep") have taken on the qualities and/ spirit of the celestial being (the "Lamb") who they share the same type of title with.

ARI'EL INSTITUTE

THE TWO GROUPS OF 144,000 IN REVELATION

BRO. J.A.R. (Mexico): Can you expand on some scriptures on the two groups of 144,000 in Revelation? Some are mentioned in **Revelation 7** and the other group is mentioned in **Revelation 14**. I understand that those in **Revelation 7** are only natural Jews and those of **Revelation 14** are men and women chosen from all over the earth to form the Bride of Christ. Can you talk on this and expand some more on it?

BRO. BAER: How you have described it is how I see it. Another reason we have used for there being two groups of 144,000 each (one who is the Bride and one who will be the future Israelite overcomers, working under Christ and the Bride) is found in a typological picture in **1 Chronicles 27**. When David set up his governors over Israel, there were 24,000 who served each month of the year (twelve months) which would make 288,000 total (24,000 x 12), which could equate to the total number of individuals in the two sets of 144,000 in Revelation (144,000 x 2 = 288,000).

BRO. J.A.R. (Mexico): Bro. Baer, what a beautiful type! Also, multiplying the twelve tribes of natural Israel and the twelve apostles gives us as a result of 144 (12 x 12 = 144). Could this have to do with the 144,000?

BRO. BAER: Bro. R., there are brethren who do make those parallels in one way or another. I do think the number twelve is significant as it often is symbolic of "government" in the Bible and 12 x 12 (12 squared) might be intended to convey a full, complete, or even perfect government. The group of 144,000 in **Revelation 7** is clearly based on this pattern of 12 x 12 (12 tribes x 12,000 members out of each). The 12 apostles might be related symbolically with the number of the Bride company, but I also believe there may be other apostles in the latter rain church as well.

BRO. M.M.: Revelation 7 starts with the angels that will pour out judgement being restrained until the 144,000 Jews are sealed. People try to say that the Jews were scattered, and you can't find that many with their true lineages. I would beg to differ. Yes, they were scattered, but who can discount the living God who says a thing will be? Remember Elijah crying on the backside of a mountain?

1 Kings 19:9-18 *And he came thither unto a cave, and lodged there; and, behold, the word of the LORD came to him, and he said unto him, What doest thou here, Elijah? And he said, I have been very jealous for the LORD God of hosts: for the children of Israel have forsaken thy covenant, thrown down thine altars, and slain* *thy prophets with the sword; and I, even I only, am left; and they seek my life, to take it away. And he said, Go forth, and stand upon the mount before the LORD. And, behold, the LORD passed by, and a great and strong wind rent the mountains, and brake in pieces the rocks before the LORD; but the LORD was not in the wind: and after the wind an earthquake; but the LORD was not in the earthquake: And after the earthquake a fire; but the LORD was not in the fire: and after the fire a still small voice. And it was so, when Elijah heard it, that he wrapped his face in his mantle, and went out, and stood in the entering in of the cave. And, behold, there came a voice unto him, and said, What doest thou here, Elijah? And he said, I have been very jealous for the LORD God of hosts: because the children of Israel have forsaken thy covenant, thrown down thine altars, and slain thy prophets with the sword; and I, even I only, am left; and they seek my life, to take it away. And the LORD said unto him, Go, return on thy way to the wilderness of Damascus: and when thou comest, anoint Hazael to be king over Syria: And Jehu the son of Nimshi shalt thou anoint to be king over Israel: and Elisha the son of Shaphat of Abel-meholah shalt thou anoint to be prophet in thy room. And it shall come to pass, that him that escapeth the sword of Hazael shall Jehu slay: and him that escapeth from the sword of Jehu shall Elisha slay. Yet I have left me seven thousand in Israel, all the knees which have not bowed unto Baal, and every mouth which hath not kissed him.*

We shouldn't doubt the Lord can perform what he says. These Jewish men and women will take the Gospel to all people through the great tribulation and throughout the following 1,000 years. The group you see in **Revelation 14** will rule and reign with Christ for that 1,000-year period and beyond. They will no doubt be working with the Jewish ministry on the earth.

BRO. BAER. Amen Bro. M., well said.

ARI'EL INSTITUTE

IS REPLACEMENT THEOLOGY BIBLICAL?

SIS. B.F.: Is replacement theology biblical?

SIS. K.Z.: What is replacement theology? Please explain.

BRO. D.B.: It is the belief that God replaced natural Israel with spiritual Israel: the church. The disagreement is about whether God will or will not ever return natural Israel as being His chosen nation. I hope this helps.

BRO. BAER: Sis. F., by replacement theology, are you referring to the view that all of the promises and purposes of natural Israel have been forever replaced by the New Testament church? I ask because there are some more moderate versions that are called by that terminology that believe Israel is only dispensationally replaced ***until*** they are restored, and then they will be a part of the New Covenant economy of God.

SIS. B.F.: Bro. Baer, yes, I am referring to the extreme view that Israel has been eternally judged and will never be restored in any form. In doing my own research on the subject of replacement theology I have found that the extreme view is widely accepted in nominal religion, but also among some of us. While it may appear to be benign, this doctrine, is rooted in antisemitism.

BRO. BAER: Yes, Sis. F., it is becoming a more and more prevalent view in nominal Christendom. There have always been brethren among us who held this view, but to this point it has always been a very small minority. Though I would never accuse anyone holding this doctrine of antisemitism (unless they clearly demonstrated such), you are absolutely right that it was first taught, and principally has been maintained, by clearly antisemitic individuals who either had an intrinsic hatred of Jews or who developed that feeling because they were rejected in their attempts to evangelize the Jews. Most folks do not realize that is what happened to Martin Luther. He began with a restorationist position regarding Israel and thought for sure that his "new" Reformation message would finally be the message that would reach the Jews. When it failed to do so, he become virulently antisemitic.

SIS. B.F.: I have read Martin Luther's antisemitic words regarding the Jews. I had no idea that he expected the Jews to convert as a result of his Reformation movement.

BRO. BAER: There have been several like that in history who became very antisemitic after the Jews rejected their message. Muhammad was the same. He initially thought the Jews (and Christians) would accept him as the next "prophet" of God, and when they did not....

BRO. V.M.: Romans 10:12 *For there is no difference between the Jew and the Greek: for the same Lord over all is rich unto all that call upon him.*

Galatians 3:28 *There is neither Jew nor Greek, there is neither bond nor free, there is neither male nor female: for ye are all one in Christ Jesus.*

BRO. BAER: There is certainly no difference *in salvational value* now of being of one race or nationality versus another. But, that does not necessarily mean that God may not use a certain nation for a specific purpose today or in some period to come. The passages that talk about there being no difference now under the New Covenant simply mean that the opportunity for salvation is equally open to all, not just to Israel, and that all races and nations (under the New Covenant) now have equal access and opportunity to be a part of the kingdom.

Revelation 7:9 *After this I beheld, and, lo, a great multitude, which no man could number, of all nations, and kindreds, and people, and tongues, stood before the throne, and before the Lamb, clothed with white robes, and palms in their hands;*

The context of **Galatians 3:28** that you mentioned is that the Jews had been under the law of Moses for the purpose of it bringing them eventually (as a schoolmaster) to Christ, but now that Christ had come, the Mosaic law was being eclipsed by the New Covenant, and the singularity of Israel and the *only* people of God (prior to the New Covenant) was changed. Now all who are baptized into Christ (by the Holy Spirit) are equally part of the spiritual kingdom of God (regardless of race or nationality). In my opinion though, that has no bearing on specific callings within the kingdom: different callings and responsibilities that are or will be held by different groups for different purposes. I am not referring to something that is salvational in nature (meaning one group will be saved while another will not). I am referring to one group having a specialized calling and purpose that sets them apart. The statement of **Galatians 3:28** is regarding salvation now being open to all. Again, that is not saying that every calling is open to all or that there are no longer any people who have a calling that is different from others. Every person (or group of people for that matter) under the New Covenant does not have the same calling, role to play, office, etc.

Romans 10:12 is addressing exactly the same thing: equality in terms of opportunity of salvation. The very next verse makes that clear.

Romans 10:13 *For whosoever shall call upon the name of the Lord shall be saved.*

Again, this has nothing to do with specific callings or responsibilities of any person or people, it has to do with the general opportunity for salvation afforded to all people. It does not say that whosoever calls on the name of the Lord will have a ministerial office, or will be one of those who work in a specific type of calling, but simply that they will all be saved. So, if God intends for genetic Israelites to have a special role (a specific calling) in the kingdom to come, that is not at all contradicted by the passages you quoted as those passages have nothing to do with whether or not anyone might have a special calling or position of responsibility at some point, but to whom salvation is being made accessible.

BRO. F.L.S.: Jeremiah 3:8 *And I saw, when for all the causes whereby backsliding Israel committed adultery I had put her away, and given her a bill of divorce; yet her treacherous sister Judah feared not, but went and played the harlot also.*

BRO. BAER: Yes, that is what (in great part) caused her to be sent into captivity in Babylon, which is the overall context of Jeremiah's message. But, even that terrible "putting away" still had a restoration that followed it.

Jeremiah 25:8-12 *Therefore thus saith the LORD of hosts; Because ye have not heard my words, Behold, I will send and take all the families of the north, saith the LORD, and Nebuchadrezzar the king of Babylon, my servant, and will bring them against this land, and against the inhabitants thereof, and against all these nations round about, and will utterly destroy them, and make them an astonishment, and an hissing, and perpetual desolations. Moreover I will take from them the voice of mirth, and the voice of gladness, the voice of the bridegroom, and the voice of the bride, the sound of the millstones, and the light of the candle. And this whole land shall be a desolation, and an astonishment; and these nations shall serve the king of Babylon seventy years. And it shall come to pass, when seventy years are accomplished, that I will punish the king of Babylon, and that nation, saith the LORD, for their iniquity, and the land of the Chaldeans, and will make it perpetual desolations.*

Jeremiah 29:10-14 *For thus saith the LORD, That after seventy years be accomplished at Babylon I will visit you, and perform my good word toward you, in causing you to return to this place. For I know the thoughts that I think toward you,* *saith the LORD, thoughts of peace, and not of evil, to give you an expected end. Then shall ye call upon me, and ye shall go and pray unto me, and I will hearken unto you. And ye shall seek me, and find me, when ye shall search for me with all your heart. And I will be found of you, saith the LORD: and I will turn away your captivity, and I will gather you from all the nations, and from all the places whither I have driven you, saith the LORD; and I will bring you again into the place whence I caused you to be carried away captive.*

BRO. V.M.: Romans 10:1-4 *Brethren, my heart's desire and prayer to God for Israel is, that they might be saved. For I bear them record that they have a zeal of God, but not according to knowledge. For they being ignorant of God's righteousness, and going about to establish their own righteousness, have not submitted themselves unto the righteousness of God. For Christ is the end of the law for righteousness to every one that believeth.*

BRO. BAER: Yes, Bro. M., but that statement is not the end of Paul's comments on Israel in this letter. The entire eleventh chapter (immediately following what you just quoted) directly contradicts the idea that they were eternally cut off from God. It so clearly and heavily states this in so many different ways that it would be overwhelming to quote it all in one comment, but I'll just note a few of Paul's statements there.

Romans 11:11-12 *I say then, Have they stumbled that they should fall? God forbid: but rather through their fall salvation is come unto the Gentiles, for to provoke them to jealousy. Now if the fall of them be the riches of the world, and the diminishing of them the riches of the Gentiles; how much more their fulness?*

Romans 11:15-24 *For if the casting away of them be the reconciling of the world, what shall the receiving of them be, but life from the dead? For if the firstfruit be holy, the lump is also holy: and if the root be holy, so are the branches. And if some of the branches be broken off, and thou, being a wild olive tree, wert graffed in among them, and with them partakest of the root and fatness of the olive tree; Boast not against the branches. But if thou boast, thou bearest not the root, but the root thee. Thou wilt say then, The branches were broken off, that I might be graffed in. Well; because of unbelief they were broken off, and thou standest by faith. Be not highminded, but fear: For if God spared not the natural branches, take heed lest he also spare not thee. Behold therefore the goodness and severity of God: on them which fell, severity; but toward thee, goodness, if thou continue in his goodness: otherwise thou also shalt be cut off. And they also, if they abide not still in unbelief, shall be graffed in: for God is able to graff them in again. For if thou wert cut out of* *the olive tree which is wild by nature, and wert graffed contrary to nature into a good olive tree: how much more shall these, which be the natural branches, be graffed into their own olive tree?*

Romans 11:25-27 *For I would not, brethren, that ye should be ignorant of this mystery, lest ye should be wise in your own conceits; that blindness in part is happened to Israel, until the fulness of the Gentiles be come in. And so all Israel shall be saved: as it is written, There shall come out of Sion the Deliverer, and shall turn away ungodliness from Jacob: For this is my covenant unto them, when I shall take away their sins.*

Romans 11:28-29 *As concerning the gospel, they are enemies for your sakes: but as touching the election, they are beloved for the fathers' sakes. For the gifts and calling of God are without repentance.*

Romans 10 must, and can only be, taken in light of the most obvious and clear meaning of **Romans 11**, not as some separate disconnected statement. There has not been anything that has occurred in history *after* the time of the writing of Romans that could have possibly been the fulfillment of those statements. There was no great influx of the Jews into the church after that time since the influx of Jewish converts to the church had already dramatically decreased by the time of the writing of Romans. But, **Romans 11** is foretelling a great turning of the Jews to Christ in a way that was in the future to those Paul was writing to, not present or past. Any coming into the church by the Jews had nearly dried up to nothing by the time Paul wrote Romans, and there was not a revival of any kind among the people of Israel after Romans was written, and there hasn't been *yet*.

BRO. V.M.: How does it get any simpler than the statement Paul made?

Romans 10:12 *For there is no difference between the Jew and the Greek....*

BRO. BAER: It is very simple, though you may have missed its simplicity with your Preterist presuppositions. There is no difference in terms of opportunity for salvation. Salvation is no longer through the law of Moses or principally only available to the natural seed of Abraham. It is just that simple. Any other interpretation or additions to Paul's meaning is what will make it less than simple…and less than biblical as well. Arguing that this is a reference to all callings within the kingdom now being the same (and thus arguing that Israel has no specific calling or purpose God may use her for in the future) is seriously overcomplicating the meaning of these statements and is not at all what they are talking about. They are simply speaking about the opportunity for salvation and relationship with God which is now available to all regardless of race or nationality.

BRO. V.M.: The God of heaven no longer sees any distinction between a Jew or a Gentile because of the fulfillment of the law by the sacrifice of Christ. Just because one may call himself a Jew doesn't mean they are a Jew.

BRO. BAER: That is true in terms of salvational opportunity: there is no distinction. In terms of the high calling (membership in the Bride) there is no distinction: all races will be represented in the Bride (able to hold the highest offices in the kingdom). And, all races have equal opportunity to enter into the kingdom. But, that has no bearing at all on whether or not God may have a specific role and purpose for Israel (for Israelites) within the kingdom.

You are trying to take these types of statements a step further than what they actually state. Statements of this kind are simply saying that salvation is an "equal opportunity" racially, nationally, etc. Arguing that it *also*, or *instead*, means that God will never use natural Israel (genetic Israelites) for a particular role of some kind in the future is not at all what these verses are stating. It is actually quite the opposite when the whole context of what is said about the Jews is considered (especially in the book of Romans). You are adding to the simple straightforward meaning of these statements to build a case for something that is an entirely unrelated issue, and your interpretation is actually in direct contradiction to the overall message of the context of the passages you are quoting, the books they are written in, and the whole span of the scriptural testimony.

You are cherry picking out less than a handful of statements that are very simple in meaning regarding overall salvation, and reading your theology and (I pray not) potential prejudices into them by removing their meaning from their clear context and in contradiction to many other scriptures.

You may want these statements to say what you believe they do, but they simply do not, and if they did, they would directly contradict a number of other statements by the very same writer in the very same books where they are found.

BRO. V.M.: Romans 2:28-29 *For he is not a Jew, which is one outwardly; neither is that circumcision, which is outward in the flesh: But he is a Jew, which is one inwardly; and circumcision is that of the heart, in the spirit, and not in the letter; whose praise is not of men, but of God.*

BRO. BAER: Absolutely, but once again, this has nothing to do with whether or not individuals who are genetic Israelites may have a specific purpose in God's economy in the future. Rather, it is saying the same thing the other verses are: that the Jews no longer have a monopoly on salvation, and that it is no longer natural descent from Abraham that makes someone automatically (if they are circumcised and obedient to the law of Moses) part of God's kingdom. Now all who are filled with the Spirit are equally part of God's spiritual kingdom. But, once again, that has nothing to do with callings within the kingdom.

If God chose to use the United States for a specific purpose (which He certainly appears to have done) that would not contradict this verse, and if He chooses to use Israel for a specific purpose in the future, it has nothing to do with this verse's meaning either. This is not speaking about callings and purposes *within* the kingdom but is referring to general salvation and membership in the family of God through the baptism of the Spirit. In other words, someone does not have to be descended from Abraham to be a part of God's economy under the New Covenant. Being descended from Abraham does not automatically make someone a part. All now must be filled with the Spirit to be spiritual children of God. Any use God may have for Israel in the future will have to *first* be preceded by them being filled with the Spirit and restored into the kingdom of God... which they certainly are not corporately at this time.

You realize that many thousands of genetic Israelites became a part of the kingdom in the period of the early church, and if many become a part of the kingdom in the period of the latter rain church, and into the Millennial Reign, they would be in the kingdom. If a great number of Jews are in the kingdom, surely God could use them for a special purpose within the kingdom, couldn't He? They will not be able to carry out that special calling until after they have come into the kingdom though, so what is the point of arguing over whether they must be "spiritual Jews" by Holy Spirit baptism. Of course, but that does not mean that they are no longer genetic Jews because they have been filled with the Spirit. Their genetic DNA is not changed by Holy Spirit baptism. What is changed is their spiritual status of being in a relationship with God. If God wanted to use them for a special purpose (which the Bible clearly states) *after* they are restored to Him by faith in Christ and Holy Spirit baptism, why would that be so strange to comprehend?

BRO. F.L.S.: If God "remarried" Israel after divorcing her, then He would not be adhering to His own word.

Jeremiah 3:1-8 *They say, If a man put away his wife, and she go from him, and become another man's, shall he return unto her again? shall not that land be greatly polluted? but thou hast played the harlot with many lovers; yet return again to me, saith the LORD. Lift up thine eyes unto the high places, and see where thou hast not been lien with. In the ways hast thou sat for them, as the Arabian in the wilderness; and thou hast polluted the land with thy whoredoms and with thy wickedness. Therefore the showers have been withholden, and there hath been no latter rain; and thou hadst a whore's forehead, thou refusedst to be ashamed. Wilt thou not from this time cry unto me, My father, thou art the guide of my youth? Will he reserve his anger for ever? will he keep it to the end? Behold, thou hast spoken and done evil things as thou couldest. The LORD said also unto me in the days of Josiah the king, Hast thou seen that which backsliding Israel hath done? she is gone up upon every high mountain and under every green tree, and there hath played the harlot. And I said after she had done all these things, Turn thou unto me. But she returned not. And her treacherous sister Judah saw it. And I saw, when for all the causes whereby backsliding Israel committed adultery I had put her away, and given her a bill of divorce; yet her treacherous sister Judah feared not, but went and played the harlot also.*

BRO. V.M.: God ended His relationship with the Jewish people, and then He poured out His wrath and anger on Israel in the destruction of 70 A.D., the single most prophesied event in all of Scripture that was fulfilled as Jesus had prophesied.

Luke 19:41-44 *And when he was come near, he beheld the city, and wept over it, Saying, If thou hadst known, even thou, at least in this thy day, the things which belong unto thy peace! but now they are hid from thine eyes. For the days shall come upon thee, that thine enemies shall cast a trench about thee, and compass thee round, and keep thee in on every side, And shall lay thee even with the ground, and thy children within thee; and they shall not leave in thee one stone upon another; because thou knewest not the time of thy visitation.*

BRO. BAER: There is some debate by Hebrew scholars as to whether the language in the passage about this bill of divorcement was a threat of divorcement, the beginnings of what would be divorce proceedings, so to speak, or fully completed divorcement which somewhat complicates the issue of what this might be referring to. But, as I already pointed out, the very statement you are quoting regarding God, at the very least moving into divorce proceedings (so to speak), is qualified by the fact that what Jeremiah is historically referring to (at least in its initial historical fulfillment) was associated with God's judgement on Judah in Jeremiah's day. He specifically notes that what He is accusing them of includes events during king

Josiah's reign which occurred before the Babylonian captivity. The judgement God was referring to in **Jeremiah 3** was carried out (at least in part) by the destruction of Jerusalem and the Temple in 586 B.C. and the seventy-year Babylonian captivity… after which God restored Judah back to Himself, which all by itself contradicts your conclusions that the judgement He described (associated with potential divorce) in **Jeremiah 3** was a judgement that Judah could not be restored from: restored back into relationship with God at some future point. They clearly were restored back to relationship with God following that judgement.

Regardless of that, I think you brethren are entirely missing a very simple point that nullifies your whole argument that God could not "remarry" Judah if He divorced her. Since you are determined to take **Jeremiah 3** out of its historical context and apply it to present day Israel (which might be possible in a multi-layered prophetic sense, but which would not change its first historical fulfillment), let me follow you down that rabbit trail for a moment and see if it leads where you think that it does.

Have you ever considered that the Israel that God intends to enter into relationship with (as I believe it) in the future is not even the same Israel that He broke off relationship with nearly 2,000 years ago? That is true on two different levels. First of all, Israel is not some amorphous non-personal entity. Israel is a nation made up of individuals. Its constitution (makeup) changes every several generations as those who were Israel are replaced by those who are now Israel. In other words, the Israel that existed in the first century A.D. is not the same Israel (in terms of the same Israelites) that existed in the 1800's A.D., and those are not the same as the Israelites that exist today. You seem to be under the strange impression that the personal constituents who made up the nation of Israel that was judged in the first century A.D. are the very same that exist today. Yes, the nation (as an impersonal "thing") might be said to be the same, but the individuals that constitute it change. That means that even if God divorced that entire generation that was Israel in the first century, that is not necessarily synonymous with saying that he is "re-divorcing" every generation forever after that. Some might argue (and it is worth discussing) that the present nation of Israel is not divorced from God so much as they have never been married to Him to begin with. The nation that was their mother that preceded them was divorced by God, but they are the daughter of that nation. That is easily supported by the language God uses about Aholah and Aholibah (**Ezekiel 23**) or Lo-ruhamah and Lo-Ammi (**Hosea 1 – 2**), both examples of which represented the children of a harlot mother, who followed in her harlotry. The Israel that was judged of God in the first century A.D. was the mother of children who also have rejected His Messiah. Each generation of Israelites has corporately continued this, but all it will take will be one single generation of Israelites who, instead of continuing in their mother's rejection of Christ, will turn to him.

On a deeper, spiritual level though, even if it could be argued that the Israel of today is synonymous with the Israel that God divorced (which is problematic for the reasons I just gave), God could still remarry her without contradicting His prior statements at all if He was not marrying the same Israel in a spiritual sense. If Israel is born again by the Spirit, then she is no longer the same "person" He divorced. Though she was dead to Him (and death breaks the marriage vow and allows for remarriage), she can be made alive to Him. We all were in this state: cut off from God by our sins (no different than being in a spiritually divorced state), but we were born again by Spirit baptism so that we could enter into proper relationship with Him. We have to be taken out of Adam and be put in Christ, and that then makes us a *new* creature.

If it could even be argued that Israel was fully divorced from God (which is open for debate) that would be no different than the human race beginning by being in relationship with God, then falling and being cut off from God (divorced from that relationship), but still being able to enter back into a relationship with Him by the blood of Christ and by being born again of the Spirit. If the terrible rejection of God's will by mankind can be reversed by these elements, surely Israel's past and present rejection of His Son can be.

As to your quotations Bro. M., once again, they do not override the many statements that speak about restoration *after* rejection, nor does your interpretation take into consideration that even the most dire and diabolical of sins (the Fall of humanity) is capable of being reversed by *later* human beings who turn to Christ and are filled with the Spirit. All mankind was cut off from God by the Fall but that cutting off can be reversed – even by those who have rejected Him.

BRO. V.M.: What you fail to understand is many of those statements refer to the New Jerusalem, and to a spiritual Israel, and not to the destroyed natural nation of Israel. We ourselves are spiritual Jews.

Revelation 3:12 *Him that overcometh will I make a pillar in the temple of my God, and he shall go no more out: and I will write upon him the name of my God, and the name of the city of my God, which is new Jerusalem, which cometh down out of heaven from my God: and I will write upon him my new name.*

BRO. BAER: Of course we are, but again, that has no bearing on God's individual or group-specific callings and purposes, nor does it change whether or not God intends to take a group of people, for the sake of their ancient fathers, and use them in the future.

BRO. V.M.: Israel is no more but the true Israel was never meant to be the natural children of Jacob.

Romans 9:6-8 *Not as though the word of God hath taken none effect. For they are not all Israel, which are of Israel: Neither, because they are the seed of Abraham, are they all children: but, In Isaac shall thy seed be called. That is, They which are the children of the flesh, these are not the children of God: but the children of the promise are counted for the seed.*

They which are the children of the flesh are not the children of God.

BRO. M.L.: Bro. M., I think that these statements make it clear that this is just speaking of exactly what Bro. Baer is saying. There is no longer a monopoly in salvation held by the natural Jew, but it is to the Jew first and also to the Gentile (**Romans 1:16**).

Romans 9:30-32 *What shall we say then? That the Gentiles, which followed not after righteousness, have attained to righteousness, even the righteousness which is of faith. But Israel, which followed after the law of righteousness, hath not attained to the law of righteousness. Wherefore? Because they sought it not by faith, but as it were by the works of the law. For they stumbled at that stumblingstone;*

BRO. V.M.: The problem is this idea that somehow Israel still has a part in unfulfilled prophecy when in reality they were eternally judged as a nation in 70 A.D. The ramifications of that truth wreak havoc on people's interpretation of prophecy, hence their objection to "replacement theology".

BRO. BAER: Bro. M., your continued quoting of less than a handful of passages, that are referring to who God's true people (children) under the New Covenant have no bearing whatsoever on who God may use for a special purpose in the future ***after*** they have become part of His people. Continuing to quote these passages over and over again out of context and with a supposed meaning that is entirely outside their scope is not going to prove your position. Those statements have nothing whatsoever to do with whether or not God will restore the Jews at some point in the future. They are not referring to who may ***one day*** be God's people, but to who God's people are presently: *today*. Of course the Jews (as a whole) are not God's people (spiritual children) today. They cannot be until they accept Christ and are filled with the Spirit. You continue using verses that have no bearing whatsoever on the issue, and do nothing to affirm your arguments. As long as Israel remains outside the New Covenant, they are not God's people. But, that has nothing to do with whether they may be part of the people of God in the future. Anyone who has not accepted God through Christ is not one of God's people in the present, but that does not mean that they will not be at some point in the future. There are many millions who have not yet accepted Christ who will do so in the future. Presently they are not God's people, but that does not mean that they cannot become His people at some point.

EDITORIAL NOTE: Bro. M. made a number of very derogatory and pejorative statements (which are not included here).

BRO. BAER: There are certain doctrinal teachings that seem to (oddly and mysteriously) very often produce a bad spirit in those who believe them. This is one of those. By a bad spirit I mean a condescending, corrective, confrontational, argumentative, mocking, divisive, demeaning, and even angry tone that seems to be nearly always present in those who argue for these beliefs. Let me stress that I am not referring to you individually with these statements, as you have been very mild in tone in comparison to some I have encountered. But, I have never had a discussion with someone who takes your position (Preterist or similar) on this issue that has not (at some point) demonstrated that type of spirit when discussing this subject, and I have discussed it with a large number of different individuals. There is nearly always a snide, sarcastic, and sharp tone present in their arguments. There is nearly always an almost angrily dogmatic spirit to their claims. They will not budge one inch on the possibility that they may be in error regarding any of their claims on this subject…likely because one error in their tenuous interpretational "house of cards" could potentially bring the whole thing crashing down. There are several other subjects that seem to be similar: that create the same kind of spirit in many of those who hold to them, and this has always troubled me about them. If folks holding to a certain doctrinal position or interpretation are consistently conflict seekers, very often arguing for their view in a bad spirit, with discourtesy and disrespect towards those with any other view but their own... it might be worth considering whether it is the view they are espousing that is producing this type of spirit.

BRO. L.T.: The wrong recipe will not produce the right result.

BRO. BAER: Returning to the original question on replacement theology, the most extreme form of replacement theology is the teaching that natural Israel has been entirely and eternally replaced by the church, and that all of their promises and future hopes now only belong to the church. Someone who believes this holds that Israel can never be restored, which as I have been stating, is a bit odd considering their rejection of God was no different than that of Adam, and yet Adam's race, much of which is still in a state of being outside of relationship with God, will one day be fully and entirely restored back to Him.

Now, *in a way*, replacement theology is true... but only in that *until* natural Israel becomes part of spiritual Israel (the church) they are cut off from the possibility of receiving the promises God had specifically intended for them in terms of the purpose He intended them to carry out and the place He intended them to fulfill... though that is related to a role they can only fill once they become part of the spiritual kingdom of God that they were cut off from.

There is another thing to take into consideration though when taking a side on an issue of this kind. If someone is wrong about Israel being restored back to God, the salvational repercussions of that belief being wrong are minimal, if non-existent. Meaning, if someone thinks Israel will be restored and they are not, it is unlikely that belief will affect that person negatively in terms of their salvation. They simply believe (if they are wrong) and hope that more folks will be saved and used by God than will be. That certainly won't produce the wrong spirit. On the other hand, if Israel is going to be restored and someone refuses to accept that and boasts against them being grafted back in (**Romans 11:18**) that belief (if wrong) could have a major impact on a person's spirit and the development of prejudices (including racial prejudices) that could potentially be very harmful to their spirit and their salvation.

It is not only important to consider all the reasons for why we believe whatever it is we believe, it is also critical to consider the repercussions of what our beliefs might produce in our other beliefs, and in our spirit, if they are incorrect.

BRO. V.M.: Israel at a certain point in time went from a natural progeny to the spiritual entity they were always meant to be, they do not coexist. Confusion arises in determining which is being referred to in any given scripture.

BRO. BAER: Natural Israel has always been natural Israel (genetic descendants of Abraham). The fact that the majority of Abraham's genetic descendants have (thus far) chosen to reject Christ does not mean that they are no longer natural Israel. It simply means that they are not presently spiritual Israel.

BRO. V.M.: This should put this disagreement to rest and it is beyond me why it is not sufficient. I thank you for considering my position and my prayer and earnest hope is that we all come to the knowledge of the truth.

Romans 2:28 *For he is not a Jew, which is one outwardly; neither is that circumcision, which is outward in the flesh:*

BRO. BAER: It is odd to me that you would think a scripture will put a subject to rest that it is not even addressing, and I continue to remain somewhat befuddled that you are not hearing what this passage is actually saying or seeing its clear and contextual meaning. This statement has nothing at all to do with whether or not God intends some future purpose for those who are natural Israelites after they have received His Son and become His spiritual people. Of course they are not spiritual Israelites if they have not been converted and filled with the Holy Spirit. But, that has no bearing on whether or not they will be some day. You continue using this (and the two or three other similar statements in the New Testament) in a way in which they are not intended by their Author. **Romans 2** simply does not (and cannot) mean that God will never allow natural Israel to be restored to a relationship with Him through His Son at some point as that restoration is the entire thrust of the ninth through eleventh chapters of the very same book written by the very same writer. The statements you continue quoting are not even addressing whether or not Israel might have a future hope. They are only addressing who is presently spiritual Israel. A genetic Israelite who rejected Christ did not suddenly have his physical DNA adjusted so that he was no longer an Israelite. They are still physical Israelites, just not (at this time) spiritual Israelites.

BRO. V.M.: When Paul spoke these words, it was clear to the early church saints that God no longer considered natural Israel in any way. You cannot accept this truth because it would destroy so many other beliefs you retain about Israel's coming restoration, which is never going to happen.

BRO. BAER: That is entirely your opinion. The only thing that is clear biblically is that there still was a natural Israel, but that being a part of natural Israel was no longer sufficient to claim relationship with God. No one who is a natural Israelite and refuses to accept Christ is part of God's spiritual people. They are no more a child of God than any person or nation who refuses to accept Christ. But, once again, that has nothing to do with whether natural Israel will turn to Him at some point in the future. All that it means is that those who have not are not presently His spiritual people. That does not mean that they will never be in a relationship with God at some point in the future. The only verses you have to (supposedly) support your view do not support it at all. They have nothing to do with whether Israel as a nation may one day be restored. They are simply identifying who spiritual Israel presently is under the New Covenant: those who are in relationship with God through Christ and by the Spirit. Those statements have nothing to do with whether those who are natural might one day become spiritual.

Your argument falls apart when simple biblical facts and common sense are applied to it. Surely you believe that the nations will one day all become part of the kingdom of God (will turn to Christ and will submit to his rule). Israel is one of those nations after all. You are determined to redefine this language because if you are wrong, you are wrong about a good deal of your interpretations. If we are wrong about Israel's restoration the only damage done (if such could be even said to be damage) is that we believed that some folks were going to be saved who were not going to be. If you are wrong, there are far more dire consequences since you will have rejected the counsel of God regarding His future work, will have taken a stand against His future purpose, and will have developed a racial animus towards a people that God loves and intends to use.

ARI'EL INSTITUTE

OVER-ALLEGORIZED INTERPRETATIONAL METHODS

BRO. T.Z.: I think that when people overcomplicate and always "type and shadow" things it sometimes even surprises God. He said he hid these things from the wise and prudent and revealed them unto babes. Wise and prudent would also compare to the Greeks who were always looking for some new thing (**Acts 17:21**). My point is that when people go through and over complicate the Bible they may stand in error. Yes, Jesus spoke in parables but they did make sense! If you spiritualize without spiritual eyes you'll tell spiritual lies!

BRO. BAER: Well said Bro. Z. The carnal mind seems driven to always look for something deeper and more mysterious in meaning: some "new" way of looking at the Scripture that no one else has seen before. Part of the reason some are caught up in such is simple pride: wanting to have folks think highly of them and their "revelations". Part of it is the insatiable desire to keep digging rather than to (many times) actually do something with the truths you have. Some are more interested in debating their version of the "truth" than putting the real truth into shoe leather and allowing it to change their spirit and actions. I pray to God I am not in the former category, and I am striving with all I am able to be in the latter.

Jesus's parables were most often very clear in meaning to those who he wanted to get the message (which is why they responded the way they did with anger and hatred). When he spoke in parables that contained insights for his disciples, he very often took them aside and explained them in more detail. I might point out (that it is not my intent to wade into this subject) that if all his references to Satan and to his angels, or to evil spirits in the Gospels were symbolic or parabolic, they are missing both of these normal things: no one hearing them was insulted by their underlying meaning, and he never took his disciples aside to explain to them who he was (supposedly) referring to when he used titles like Satan and the Devil. Given that nearly all of the common Jews of his day believed in Satan as a spiritual entity, you would think, if Jesus was referring to him parabolically as something else entirely, he would at least have taken his disciples aside and explained that (as he did with other parabolic language at times) since some of them (if not all of them) would have seen him as a personal entity if they believed anything like the vast majority of the common Jews of their day.

Some interpretations that are overly allegorical and excessive in their rewriting of the most obvious meaning of the Scripture are simply the product of someone thinking they are seeing something with "spiritual eyes" (as you said) when they are actually seeing through carnal eyes. This is far more likely with excessive allegorical interpretation as allegoric and figurative interpretations are by definition far easier to create based on arbitrary methods of interpretation (picking what you want something to be allegorical of) and subjective inspiration: thinking the Spirit of God has revealed something to you that, if you truly knew the word of God (comprehensively: all of it) and technically (the biblical languages, grammar, etc.), you would know could not be true. When over-use of allegorical interpretation is being practiced, it is often motivated by the human hunger to see something deeper than everyone else: to know a (supposed) "mystery" most can't see. That might be driven by a love for the truth, or it could be driven by pride and a desire for adulation. Sometimes the reason that most can't see some person's supposedly deep spiritual insight is because it simply isn't there to see except by those who have had their eyes blurred by false presuppositions, their minds aggravated by improper methods of interpretation or incorrect use of language and grammar, and their presuppositions maintained by a strong prejudice against any other possibility (than that which they have chosen to believe).

BRO. D.P. (Canada): I have also noticed that Bro. Baer. It is an insatiable desire to please itself, by thinking these so-called deeper thoughts are what God and His Spirit are pleased in. But, it really can be carnal imagination.

BRO. BAER: I readily admit that it is very difficult (for all of us) to do, but we must establish truth based on the actual evidence and not on our assumptions (subjective ideas) and emotions (personal feelings). We must let the facts influence our feelings and not allow our feelings to influence the facts.

This is why it is so critical to have both the word and the Spirit as witnesses to the truth. Many have thought that it was the Spirit that lead them into the (supposed) "truths" they believe that, unfortunately, the word of God simply does not support. The solution to the self-deception of believing something that is wrong cannot be wrong because you are certain it was given to you by spiritual "revelation", is to consider any spiritual revelation (that may or may not be such) in light of comprehensive general study of the word of God (all that it says on a subject) and by careful technical study of the word of God (what the Hebrew and Greek words, grammar, idiomatic expressions, etc.) actually means.

It is a biblical fact that there are both actual and allegorical expressions contained in the Scripture. Sometimes one or the other is meant in a statement, and sometimes a statement contains both, but in no case is potentially subjective allegorical interpretation intended to overwrite or entirely change the clearest and most consistent, biblically based meanings of titles, words, and expressions. No matter how strongly our prejudicial presumptions have taken hold of our mind, no interpretation of the Scripture can ever contradict the Scripture itself. If a title or word is used to mean only one thing throughout the entire Scripture, no matter how hard it is for a person to accept that usage and meaning, they must do so, or they will develop implacably entrenched false ideas and simply unbiblical interpretive methods that will lead them deeper and deeper into man-made "truths" and will progressively blind them to the clear meaning of the actual biblical truth. And, the deeper we go in developing "truths" that are not actually biblically true, and the more we reinforce them with layer after layer of incorrect allegorical connections or just slightly offset (from what it actually true) interpretations, the more we will convince ourselves that what we are seeing is the product of the Spirit, when it is actually the product of our spirit. We can become oblivious to this because we have unwittingly (and perhaps unknowingly) built layer upon layer of meaning (allegorical, figurative, based on false facts, or just entirely fanciful) between our assumptions and the actual, obvious, clear truth on the surface that we have just mentally dived too "deep" below to see anymore.

ARI'EL INSTITUTE

THE CURSES IN GENESIS 3

SIS. B.F.: Are there three curses in **Genesis 3**? I only see two: the serpent is cursed, and the ground is cursed. The Lord does not use the word "cursed" with Eve. In fact, there is a promise given to Eve that is not given to Adam.

BRO. D.P.: I see the promise being made through Eve, but to (or for) all of mankind.

BRO. S.S.: Adam was cursed to work by the sweat of his brow. Eve was cursed to deliver her offspring in pain. These are two very real and definite curses. Eve's curse is in **Genesis 3:16** and Adam's curse in is **Genesis 3:19**.

Genesis 3:16 *Unto the woman he said, I will greatly multiply thy sorrow and thy conception; in sorrow thou shalt bring forth children; and thy desire shall be to thy husband, and he shall rule over thee.*

Genesis 3:19 *In the sweat of thy face shalt thou eat bread, till thou return unto the ground; for out of it wast thou taken: for dust thou art, and unto dust shalt thou return.*

BRO. BAER: The description of what Eve will undergo in childbirth and in her relationship with her husband is normally taken as part of her curse. In a more general sense, the fact that the Bible refers to the creation being under the "curse" and eventually there being no more "curse" alludes to the curse of sin and death that came upon both Adam and Eve (and all their descendants).

SIS. B.F.: The text indicates that her pain would be "multiplied", seems to indicate that she would have had pain regardless of her sin, just not as intense. The Lord does not say that Eve has been cursed as he does regarding the land and the serpent who is to go on his belly.

BRO. S.S.: In **Genesis 3:16** when the scripture says "unto the woman..." this is simply a continuation of what God is doing in the previous scripture.

BRO. BAER: The Hebrew literally says "multiplying, I will multiply", which many Hebrew scholars take to mean "I will multiply thy sorrows, and multiply those sorrows with other sorrows", which could mean (as many take it) that pain in delivery was one of those "other sorrows" that were part of the whole package of sorrows she would receive, not so much that she would necessarily have been enduring pain and now would have more pain, but that the pain of childbirth was one of the number of sorrows she would undergo (multiplied in number of sorrows rather than in the intensity of any one particular sorrow).

SIS. B.F.: Bro. Baer, yes, I agree. Sorrows verses pain. That is my understanding as well.

BRO. BAER: My basis for applying the curse to each is that though the word "cursed" may only be used for the ground and the serpent, the Bible elsewhere applies it (whether directly or indirectly) to humankind (and the whole creation) as something inherited from Adam and Eve, meaning that they were the first who were cursed, and that curse passed from them down to their descendants. The point being that Adam, Eve, the serpent, and the ground (the earth) all appear to have been cursed at this time. Adam and Eve's curse partially includes the things God told them they would suffer.

BRO. D.D.P.: Sis. F., I believe the "curse" on Eve regarding childbirth isn't so much the physical pain women endure, but the pain that comes from the knowledge the child is born into sin. I'm sure Eve's pain was multiplied when Cain killed Abel. the Bible does say "sorrow", not "pain".

BRO. BAER: That is worthy of consideration.

ARI'EL INSTITUTE

PRAYING TO AND WORSHIPING JESUS

BRO. B.Y.: Some say we are not to pray to Jesus or even to worship him. I'm just wondering have I been praying wrong my entire life. I see many verses that support this. Please help me.

BRO. BAER: I have heard some of these types of arguments myself... though I think they may be ill considered. I do believe a person can pray to Jesus and worship him as well. It is important though to understand the difference between the Almighty God (the Father) and Jesus the Son of God. Each must hold their proper place. What we should not do is to interact with the Son of God as the Almighty God. He must be interacted with and honored for who *he* is, and not as who God his Father is.

BRO. D.C.: Hebrews 4:14-16 *Seeing then that we have a great high priest, that is passed into the heavens, Jesus the Son of God, let us hold fast our profession. For we have not an high priest which cannot be touched with the feeling of our infirmities; but was in all points tempted like as we are, yet without sin. Let us therefore come boldly unto the throne of grace, that we may obtain mercy, and find grace to help in time of need.*

BRO. BAER: Amen. His mediatorial role is not impersonal and "in name only". He is our personal mediator and priestly intercessor, which means that God his Father has given him a place wherein he can be interacted with in the ways you are describing.

One of the problems is that many folks (including most Tritheists and Modalists) do not rightly understand how the words (in Hebrew and Greek) for worship are actually used in the Bible. This is not because they aren't intelligent or educated enough to know better but usually because they don't even consider the different uses of these words because they do not coincide with their already predetermined conceptions about the subject.

The Hebrew and Greek words used for "worship", including the very word that God says is the "worship" that is to be given to no other than Him (the Hebrew word *shakhah* in **Exodus 34:14**), are used for acts of reverence or honor given to individuals in the Bible *other than* God Himself that God permits and appears to even support. This is what some don't understand or don't consider. Only the Almighty God is to receive the honor and obeisance (the meanings of the Hebrew word *shakhah* often translated "worship") due to the Almighty God. In other words, only the Almighty God is to be honored and reverenced *as* the Almighty God and no one is to replace Him in that position. That has no bearing on whether or not other beings can be honored and reverenced (with the very same words translated "worship") *if* they are being honored and reverenced for the positions God has given them or allowed them to hold (and not as the Almighty God).

There are many examples of this in the Bible: places where those other than the Almighty God receive "worship" (honor, reverence, obeisance) for the high positions they hold, though *not* as or in place of the Almighty God. He appears to permit this kind of reverence to be given to others if it is given for their position and place of honor and not in place of or as His position and place of honor. One simple example is found in **1 Chronicles 29** where *both* the Almighty God and king David are "worshipped" by the people of Israel. David was not to be reverenced as the Almighty God, but as the king the Almighty God had appointed and anointed, and thus this was appropriate reverence.

1 Chronicles 29:20 *And David said to all the congregation, Now bless the LORD your God. And **all the congregation** blessed the LORD God of their fathers, and bowed down their heads, and **worshipped the LORD, and the king**.*

Both the Almighty God and king David were given "worship" (reverence, obeisance, honor), but *not* as the same person or for the same place of honor. God was worshipped as the Almighty God, and He alone is only to be worshipped as the Almighty God. David was "worshipped" as the king that God Himself gave his place of honor and not as the Almighty God.

Properly understanding this simple point completely clarifies the issue of what it means when Christ is worshipped in the Scripture: he is being given honor and glory as the Messiah and King of Kings that God his Father appointed him to be given (just like David was given this kind of honor in a lesser sense as the king that God appointed to that position and to receive that kind of honor). Jesus is not being worshipped as the one who made him Lord and Christ (**Acts 2:36**). He is appointed to receive worship because he was made Lord and Christ.

Thus… we can pray to (appeal to, communicate with, etc.) Jesus as the mediator and intercessor that God Himself has given to us, just like (in a much lesser way) someone could have fallen before and appealed to king David as the one whom God appointed and anointed as king over Israel (and several people did that very thing in the Bible).

BRO. B.Y.: Bro. Baer, thank you so much for helping me to understand. I feel so happy to understand the Scripture. I feel so blessed. I feel the Holy Ghost. I really feel great joy now.

BRO. S.S.: We can worship and pray to Jesus, while always having an understanding that we can also petition God directly with our thoughts and prayers as well. God and His son are a team, and knowing that they both hear our prayers gives peace and comfort.

BRO. S.I.S.: Yes, **John 15:16** mentions the Father in Jesus' name, and **John 17:3** lets us know we need both the Father and Son to receive eternal life. Under the New Covenant, God will not save a soul without the person accepting His Son as Lord and Savior also.

John 14:13-14, Hebrews 1:6, Revelation 5:11-12, and 7:9-10 all prove that praying to and worshiping God's only begotten Son is biblical and permitted by His Father, the Almighty God. Jesus never stopped anyone from worshiping him and when the rabbis demanded that Jesus stop them, he refused. Jesus told us in **John 5:23** that if we do not honor him as we do his Father we are not honoring the Father. The Greek word *timao* translated "honor" includes the definition "venerate," which by definition includes "worship."

BRO. BAER: I agree. His Father has given him a position that merits that level of honor.

BRO. V.M.: You have been taught wrong through no fault of your own and even now many will resist the truth, that's why falsehood flourishes among us.

Bro. Baer, are we directed in scripture to worship or pray to anyone but the Father?

BRO. BAER: As I previously pointed out, the word for "worship" used for the worship of God that is forbidden to any other is used in a number of occasions for worship that God allows and even appears to instigate others to receive. The Hebrew word translated "worship" as related to the worship given to Him is exactly the same word used for worship, honor, etc. given to king David and to others whom God appointed. It is not a different word (one word meaning "honor" and another meaning "worship"). It is the very same word for the very same thing… with one major difference. Worship and honor given to God *as the Almighty God* is only to be given to Him, while worship and honor given to others can be given to them in the role they fill, though never as the Almighty God.

This is one of the problems with not properly understanding or comprehensively studying the original language (and I have seen it many times). We can start to create improper definitions and multiple meanings of words that simply are not biblical based on our own conceptions or on looking at a translation where one single Hebrew or Greek word is translated in multiple ways (and we do not realize that fact because we have not looked at what the Hebrew or Greek words are). The word "worship" in Hebrew is used for both God (as the Almighty God) and men (as those in high positions God has appointed them to or allowed them to hold). Properly understanding this helps to clarify the nature of the Godhead and explains how Jesus can receive worship without being the Almighty God.

Jesus has been appointed to a position that is worthy of "worship": honor, glory, obeisance, etc. (all of which are meanings of the words translated "worship" in the Bible). There are numerous examples of him being appropriately worshipped as the Son of God and Messiah, though *not* as the Almighty God. No other being but the Almighty God is to be worshipped as the Almighty God, but other beings who God raises up and puts in positions of great glory and honor do receive "worship" (the exact same Hebrew word for "worship" used for worshipping God alone as God). If your argument is that he is not worshipped as the Almighty God, then you are right, but arguing that he is not intended and allowed by God to receive "worship" as the Son of God (as the Lord Christ: the Lord Messiah) is in no way biblical. There are numerous biblical examples of this.

The magi from the east "worshipped" Christ in **Matthew 2:2** and **2:11**. A leper seeking healing from Christ "worshipped" him in **Matthew 8:2**. Jairus (a ruler of the synagogue) "worshipped" Jesus before making his appeal for his daughter's life in **Matthew 9:18**. After Jesus walked on the sea and stilled the wind, the disciples "worshipped" him in **Matthew 14:33**, saying, "Of a truth thou are the Son of God" (note that the disciples did not worship him as God, but as the Son of God). The Canaanite woman whose daughter was vexed with a devil "worshipped" him when she appealed to him for his help in **Matthew 15:25**. The mother of James and John "worshipped" him when she made her request for her sons in **Matthew 20:20**. When the ladies returning from the empty tomb encountered him in **Matthew 28:9**, they "held him by the feet, and worshipped him". When the disciples saw Jesus after his resurrection in **Matthew 28:17**, they "worshipped" him. The devil possessed man in **Mark 5:6** "worshipped" him. The Roman soldiers mockingly "worshipped" him in **Mark 15:19**. The disciples who encountered Jesus after his resurrection in **Luke 24:52** "worshipped" him. The blind man who Jesus had healed "worshipped" him in **John 9:38**. The angels of God were commanded to "worship" Christ in **Hebrews 1:6**.

God Himself exalted Jesus and gave him a name and a position that makes him worthy of the level of honor and glory he has received and will receive.

Philippians 2:9-11 *Wherefore **God also hath highly exalted him, and given him a name which is above every name**: That at the name of Jesus every knee should bow, of things in heaven, and things in earth, and things under the earth; And that every tongue should confess that Jesus Christ is Lord, to the glory of God the Father.*

Revelation 5:11-14 *And I beheld, and I heard the voice of many angels round about the throne and the beasts and the elders: and the number of them was ten thousand times ten thousand, and thousands of thousands; Saying with a loud voice, **worthy is the Lamb that was slain to receive power, and riches, and wisdom, and strength, and honour, and glory, and blessing**. And every creature which is in heaven, and on the earth, and under the earth, and such as are in the sea, and all that are in them, heard I saying, **blessing, and honour, and glory, and power, be unto him that sitteth upon the throne, and unto the Lamb for ever and ever**. And the four beasts said, Amen. And the four and twenty elders fell down and worshipped him that liveth for ever and ever.*

BRO. V.M.: Revelation 22:8-13 *And I John saw these things, and heard them. And when I had heard and seen, I fell down to worship before the feet of the angel which shewed me these things. Then saith he unto me, See thou do it not: for I am thy fellowservant, and of thy brethren the prophets, and of them which keep the sayings of this book: worship God. And he saith unto me, Seal not the sayings of the prophecy of this book: for the time is at hand. He that is unjust, let him be unjust still: and he which is filthy, let him be filthy still: and he that is righteous, let him be righteous still: and he that is holy, let him be holy still. And, behold, I come quickly; and my reward is with me, to give every man according as his work shall be. I am Alpha and Omega, the beginning and the end, the first and the last.*

BRO. BAER: The Almighty God (the Father) is the *final* object of all prayer and all worship, but that has no bearing on whether or not there are beings who He allows to receive worship or appoints to positions worthy of worship. Quoting verses that disallow *certain* types of worship for *certain* individuals has no bearing on this, and it does not erase the many examples of worship being rightly received by those other than God, especially the many I just gave you regarding the worship of Christ, including **Hebrews 1:6** where God Himself commanded the angels to worship Christ. You cannot simply quote a verse to obviate dozens of other verses that clearly contradict your interpretation of that one single verse. It is a simple fact that the Bible contains numerous examples (I just gave you a number of them) of Jesus (and even king David) being worshiped and honored with the very same word for this being offered to God, in their roles and by allowance of God, though not as the Almighty God.

BRO. V.M.: You have not answered my original question. Give me a yes or no.

BRO. BAER: Apparently a long list of scriptures that answers your question (and contradicts your conclusion) is not actually a direct answer? What answer did you believe I was giving by quoting them my friend? My answer is given by the testimony of the Scripture. Shouldn't that be the best answer? Yes, Jesus is clearly given worship and communicated with in prayer as well. The Bible itself is the answer. But, perhaps some additional examples are necessary since the many already given are not sufficient for you.

1 Corinthians 1:2 *Unto the church of God which is at Corinth, to them that are sanctified in Christ Jesus, called to be* **saints, with all that in every place call upon the name of Jesus Christ our Lord***, both theirs and ours:*

The phrase translated "call upon" is the Greek *epikaléomai*. It is used to refer to audibly addressing someone. Not merely using their name, but using it in an address *to* them. There are a number of examples in the Bible of this exact kind of language used for individuals directly addressing Jesus in heaven (after he had returned to God his Father).

Acts 7:59 *And they stoned Stephen,* **calling upon** *God,* **and saying, Lord Jesus***, receive my spirit.*

The word "God" in this verse is in italics in the *King James Version* which, as I know you know, means that it was not in the original Greek. Thus, this clearly states that Stephen is calling upon Jesus in this prayer. This exact same word is used to refer to "calling on" the Father in prayer, proving that "calling on" **both** the Father and Son is appropriate:

1 Peter 1:17 *And **if ye call on the Father**, who without respect of persons judgeth according to every man's work, pass the time of your sojourning here in fear:*

The bottom line is that any and all communication addressed to Jesus is also received by God his Father. God is always the end object in one sense or another.

Paul had a direct conversation with Jesus in **Acts 9**, that included the very language of prayer:

Acts 9:3-6 *And as he journeyed, he came near Damascus: and suddenly there shined round about him a light from heaven: And he fell to the earth, and heard a voice saying unto him, Saul, Saul, why persecutest thou me? And he said, Who art thou, Lord? And* ***the Lord said, I am Jesus*** *whom thou persecutest: it is hard for thee to kick against the pricks. And he trembling and astonished said,* ***Lord, what wilt thou have me to do****? And the Lord said unto him, Arise, and go into the city, and it shall be told thee what thou must do.*

This is prayer defined. It is communication with a heavenly being that is even asking for direction from that being. Later in **Acts 9:10-14**, Ananias communicates directly with Jesus regarding this very issue, once again demonstrating this kind of direct line of communication between the saints and the Lord Jesus.

Another *possible* example of this is in **2 Corinthians 12**.

2 Corinthians 12:7-10 *And lest I should be exalted above measure through the abundance of the revelations, there was given to me a thorn in the flesh, the messenger of Satan to buffet me, lest I should be exalted above measure. For this thing I besought the Lord thrice, that it might depart from me. And he said unto me, My grace is sufficient for thee: for my strength is made perfect in weakness. Most gladly therefore will I rather glory in my infirmities, that the power of Christ may rest upon me. Therefore I take pleasure in infirmities, in reproaches, in necessities, in persecutions, in distresses for Christ's sake: for when I am weak, then am I strong.*

Almost all students of the Bible understand the title "Lord" here to be referring to the Lord Jesus Christ who Paul "besought" (prayed and appealed to) to remove this thorn. The reasons for this are very compelling as the grammar and language of the passage points to the one who is speaking and saying "my strength is made perfect" as being the one who is Christ, as the "strength" that is made perfect here is linguistically tied to the "power of Christ" that rests upon Paul.

Added to all these examples I have given is the fact that all through Jesus' ministry he is directly being appealed to for healing, help, etc. That is precisely the same kind of appeal that would constitute "prayer" for help or healing if he were not physically present (as is the case today).

The next to the last verse in the entire Bible is an example of this.

Revelation 22:20 *He which testifieth these things saith, Surely I come quickly. Amen.* **even so, come, Lord Jesus**.

BRO. C.S.: Everything that Jesus has was **given** to him by his Father. In **Matthew 28:18**, after his resurrection, he says, "All power is **given** to me in heaven and in earth." Jesus is a part of our connection to God. He is our "mediator" (**1 Timothy 2:5**). Paul said that saints of God "in every place call upon the name of Jesus Christ" (**1 Corinthians 1:2**). When Stephen was martyred, he saw Jesus and called out to him and prayed, "Lord Jesus receive my spirit" and "Lord lay not this sin to their charge" (**Acts 7:59-60**).

I'm in agreement that most biblical prayers are offered to the Father but Jesus most certainly has a part in our prayers.

John 14:13-14 *And* **whatsoever ye shall ask in my name, that will I do**, *that the Father may be glorified in the Son. If ye shall ask any thing in my name,* **I will do it**.

Bro. V.M., what do you think **Hebrews 1:6** means when it says, "let all of the angels of God worship him"? What does it mean in **Matthew 2:11** when it says that when the wise men came to the baby Jesus, "they fell down and worshiped him"? During the ministry of Jesus, we are told on multiple times that Jesus was worshiped. **Matthew 8:2, 9:18,** and **15:25** are just a few examples. At least offer some explanation of what this means to you. Thank you.

Philippians 2:9 *Wherefore God also hath highly exalted him, and given him a name which is above every name:*

Is that worship or something else?

Revelation 5:13 *Every creature which is in heaven, and on the earth and under the earth.. I heard saying, Blessing and honor, and glory, and power, be unto him that sitteth on the throne* **AND** *unto the Lamb for ever and ever.*

What does that mean?

BRO. V.M.: What does this mean?

Exodus 34:14 *For thou shalt worship no other god: for the LORD, whose name is Jealous, is a jealous God:*

BRO. C.S.: Again Bro. M., no reply to the verses that have been brought up. I will reply to **Exodus 34:14**. There was to be no heathen god, idol, or man that was to be in a place of worship in Israel.

Now what do the verses that show Jesus worshipped mean? It becomes futile discussing this with you when you never address or give your explanation of the scriptures that rebuff your argument.

BRO. V.M.: Matthew 4:10 *Then saith Jesus unto him, Get thee hence, Satan: for it is written, Thou shalt worship the Lord thy God, and him only shalt thou serve.*

BRO. C.S.: Again, no explanation of the verses given that refute your interpretation of this type of passage. You must believe that those verses mean something, don't you?

BRO. V.M.: Thou shalt worship the LORD thy God and him only shalt thou serve.

BRO. BAER: Bro. M., continuing to quote verses that refer to only worshipping God while the brethren have been giving you numerous examples of verses that refer to individuals giving a similar homage and reverence to Jesus does not disprove the meaning of those verses. It requires an explanation of them that you have not given, and simply quoting verses that appear to (by your teaching) contradict other verses in the Bible is certainly not sufficient to prove your point. We have explained how those apparent contradictions (that God is only to be worshipped and that those other than God are intended or allowed by Him to receive that same kind of homage) can be harmonized. In contrasts, you simply keep quoting one side of the issue (that God alone is to receive homage as God) without ever addressing or harmonizing the other side of the issue (that God does intend or allow others to receive homage) or, apparently, even recognizing that the second types of examples are found throughout the Bible.

Both types of statements are unquestionably found in the Bible. There is a very simple way to harmonize both though. When their full context and the overall testimony of the Scripture is considered, it is clear that commands to worship only the Lord God are referring to the fact the He alone is to be worshipped as the Almighty God.

The words translated "worship" (the Hebrew word **shakhah,** the Greek word **proskuneo**, etc.) also refer to paying homage, obeisance, and deference to one who is in a higher position or place of power and authority, whether God or human beings.

No one is to be given the homage due only to God as God, but others can be given homage (the very same words for "worship" in the Hebrew and Greek) in regard to the positions they hold. Jesus is given homage as the Son of God who is the highest agent of the Almighty God (and thus can be "worshipped" as such, as the words translated "worship" simply mean "homage", "obeisance", etc.). We are not giving him homage as the Almighty God, but as the Almighty God's highest agent, who was appointed by God to that position and given a place worthy of worship (homage) that was intended as such by God Himself. If we did give him homage as the Almighty God (as our Tritheist and Modalist brethren do), ***then*** we would be breaking the commandment not to worship any as God (the Almighty God) who is not God (the Almighty God), which is exactly what those commandments are talking about. God has given His Son Jesus a name and a position deserving of honor, glory, and worshipful deference, but it is not His own position (as the Almighty God). When we honor Christ in the position he holds (given to him by his Father) we are not dishonoring the Father by doing so (quite the opposite). We are honoring the one who God the Father intended for us to honor for the position and place he holds in the economy of God's government and order, just as the people in **1 Chronicles 29:20** (that I mentioned earlier) "worshipped" (gave honor and homage to) ***both*** the Lord God ***and*** David the king.

ARI'EL INSTITUTE

VARIANT VIEWS ON "MOVING OUT A LIVE SOUL"

BRO. W.M.: I have heard so much about "moving out a living soul". Please help me some one if you will. I know of no one that has done this as of yet. If I were to say this person or that person "moved out a live soul" would I be in error by doing such a thing? Wouldn't it take an overcomer in order to have such knowledge? Now, if anyone who is reasonable would care to state your belief about this subject please do so.

BRO. L.T.: I personally do not believe it possible for a soul to have consciousness without a body. I use the computer analogy. The computer hardware is akin to the body. The software (data) is akin to the soul. But, none of it does anything without the electricity, which is like the spirit of life that animates it all. It takes all three to have consciousness and being.

Genesis 2:7 *And the LORD God formed man of the dust of the ground, and breathed into his nostrils the breath of life; and man became a living soul.*

1 Corinthians 15:38 *But God giveth it a body as it hath pleased him, and to every seed his own body.*

BRO. B.E.: Depending on whether you believe the seals haven't been opened or if they are future dispensations, the souls under the altar in the fifth seal cried out. Did they have a body? Paul said that this earthly body would be dissolved but we have another house not made with hands (**2 Corinthians 5:1**). They weren't on earth and they had consciousness!

BRO. L.T.: Hebrews 11:4 *By faith Abel offered unto God a more excellent sacrifice than Cain, by which he obtained witness that he was righteous, God testifying of his gifts: and by it he being dead yet speaketh.*

BRO. M.L. (South Africa): The simple fact that nothing was put under the altar in the Old Testament (except ashes beside the altar which could be taken as being under the altar since the altar was raised) is proof that "souls under the altar" is symbolic language. What is this altar? Where is this altar? How big is this altar that holds the souls of all the saints?

BRO. L.T.: Yes, it is symbolic, not literal.

BRO. B.W.O. (Uganda): Leviticus 1:16 *And he shall pluck away his crop with his feathers, and cast it beside the altar on the east part, by the place of the ashes:*

This Scripture shows us that the ashes of the sacrifice were placed at the foot of, or at the base of, the altar (on the east side).

Leviticus 6:10-11 *And the priest shall put on his linen garment, and his linen breeches shall he put upon his flesh, and take up the ashes which the fire hath consumed with the burnt offering on the altar, and he shall put them beside the altar. And he shall put off his garments, and put on other garments, and carry forth the ashes without the camp unto a clean place.*

The ashes beside the altar, in type, is what John sees in **Revelation 6:9**. The burnt offering of the martyrs of Jesus Christ laid to rest at the foot of the altar in the court: laid to rest with their hearts directed "into the love of God, and into the patient waiting for Christ" (**2 Thessalonians 3:5** and **1 Thessalonians 1:10**).

The souls under the altar "speak" even as "the voice of thy brother's blood crieth unto me from the ground" (**Genesis 4:10**). Abel did not speak literally after Cain slew him. The statement that his blood cried out is figurative. The souls in **Revelation 6:9** are not alive under the golden altar in the Holy Place but, in type, they are the ashes beside the brazen altar in the court. At the first resurrection the Lord Jesus Christ in His glory will return for these ashes! **Leviticus 6:11** shows us that after the priest changes his garments, he returns for the ashes beside the altar, and carries them into a clean place. Jesus Christ has changed his garments and he is now in his glory. He is coming again out from the Holy of Holies, third heaven itself, through the holy place, back to the court for the ashes at the side of the altar, and he is going to take them back with him "unto a clean place!"

BRO. W.M.: Bro. O., please define the golden altar. We all know gold is a type of perfection. The altar is a place of sacrifice. The sacrifice had to be perfect; without spot or blemish. Those that shed their blood in the name of Jesus that were perfect were placed under the golden altar. The golden altar is a time period or dispensation during the early rain church roughly forty years where the church operated (fully). As the apostles died off there was no one to lead the sheep and by and by the church fell away when inferior men begin to sow false doctrine.

The golden altar has baffled many a soul but those under the golden altar are those that die as overcomers. They are dead but God will remember them, and they will rise and be with Christ, and they which are alive and remain will be changed and caught up to meet them in the air.

BRO. V.M.: John 11:26 *And whosoever liveth and believeth in me shall never die. Believest thou this?*

BRO. M.L. (South Africa): Hebrews 9:27 *And as it is appointed unto men once to die, but after this the judgment:*

Revelation 2:11 *He that hath an ear, let him hear what the Spirit saith unto the churches; He that overcometh shall not be hurt of the **second death**.*

Revelation 20:6 *Blessed and holy is he that hath part in the first resurrection: on such the **second death** hath no power, but they shall be priests of God and of Christ, and shall reign with him a thousand years.*

BRO. T.G.: Then who could this have been and what body did this person have in this following verse:

Revelation 22:9 *Then saith he unto me, See thou do it not: for I am thy fellowservant, and of thy brethren the prophets, and of them which keep the sayings of this book: worship God.*

BRO. BAER: Though I am presently observing rather than heavily interacting on this, I do want to point out that this passage (and its parallel in **Revelation 19:10**) may have some issues of poor translation that can make what it says sound as if it is saying something it is not. In the original Greek these passages do not actually state or even infer that this "angel" is a human believer.

Revelation 19:10 (NASB): *I am a fellow servant of yours and your brethren who hold the testimony of Jesus....*
Revelation 19:10 (ESV): *I am a fellow servant with you and your brothers who hold to the testimony of Jesus.*

The Greek underlying these statements is not actually saying that the angel is someone who is ***holding*** the testimony of Jesus, but that he is one who is a fellow servant (of the Lord) ***like*** John and his brethren who hold the testimony of Jesus. It is not saying that he is similar to them in holding the testimony of Jesus (as humans who have received the Gospel, so to speak), but that he is similar to them in being a servant of the Lord. And, even if it did (which the grammar does not really allow) intend this to mean that he had the testimony of Jesus, that wouldn't prove it was a human being as there is no reason a celestial being could not be said to have the testimony of Jesus: knowing who Jesus is and testifying to it.

Revelation 22:9 *I am a fellow servant of yours and of your brethren the prophets and of those who heed the words of this book.*

Revelation 22:9 (ESV) *I am a fellow servant **with** you and your brothers the prophets, and **with** those who keep the words of this book.*

The Greek language of this statement is also not saying the angel *is* one of John's brethren or one of the prophets but that he is a servant of the Lord just *like* those who are John's brethren and those who are the prophets are servants of the Lord. Again, this does not make him one of their human brethren or one of the human prophets, but simply one who is a servant of the Lord like they are.

These types of passages are why I keep stressing that we have to have the anointing of the Spirit *and* a knowledge of the word that is at times technical (in terms of properly understanding the original language, grammar, etc.). This is necessary in part because the English forms used by the *King James Version* translators can be misleading to those of us speaking or reading twenty-first century English. In this case, what they actually wrote may be misunderstood because of the way they wrote it, but the fact is that the Greek grammar that they based their translation on does not make this angel ***one of*** the brethren and prophets along with John and other human believers. It makes him a fellow servant of the Lord like John and his human brethren are also servants of the Lord. Both celestial and terrestrial beings are referred to as servants of the Lord. So, rightly read with proper grammar, these passages do not state or even infer that this angel was a human being in heaven.

As to the 24 elders (which are also often used to argue that human believers were already in heaven at the time of John's writing of Revelation), let me repeat some points we talked about some time back. One of the questions at that time was whether the 24 elders were human beings or celestial beings. Some of the reasons why I (and others) believe they are more likely to be celestial beings follow:

Both human beings *and* celestial beings are described as wearing white garments. Celestial beings are described in this way in **Matthew 28:3, John 20:12, Mark 16:5, Acts 1:10, Revelation 15:6,** and **Daniel 10:5-6**.

John saw the 24 elders. If they included the apostles (which is one of the standard claims made by those who believe they were human beings) wouldn't he have been among them?

It is unlikely (logically and chronologically) that Bride members would be enthroned before their Bridegroom Christ has even been declared worthy to rule as described in **Revelation 5:8-9** and before it appears that the Marriage Supper in **Revelation 19** has even occurred. Why would some of the Bride company be with the Bridegroom in a description that looks like they have already received their Bride position when the whole Bride company has not even been made up yet, and the Marriage Supper, which is part of what will formally make overcomers part of the Bride (married to Christ) has not even occurred yet?

The Greek grammar of the majority and the oldest of the Greek manuscripts of **Revelation 5:10** actually implies that the elders *do not* consider themselves as being among the humans singing the song of the redeemed. The Greek use of the pronouns "we" and "us" in the *King James Version* translation of **Revelation 5:9-10** may not be correct. The use of those pronouns is based on much later Greek manuscripts of Revelation. The oldest Greek manuscripts of Revelation (closest to the time of its original writing) actually use pronouns referring to the 24 elders as someone *other than* the human redeemed. The translation of the *New American Standard Bible* (and most other technical translations) is a good example of what the pronouns actually are in the oldest manuscripts and demonstrates why the 24 elders are likely referring to someone *other than* the human redeemed (and thus must be celestial beings that are part of the government of God in heaven).

Revelation 5:9–10 (NASB) *And they* (the 24 elders) *sang a new song, saying, Worthy are You* (Jesus) *to take the book and to break its seals; for You* (Jesus) *were slain, and purchased* (human beings) *for God with Your blood men from every tribe and tongue and people and nation. You have made **them** (human beings) to be a kingdom and priests to our God; and **they** (human beings) will reign upon the earth.*

Thus, the 24 elders are singing a song that is referring to people *other than* themselves who are the redeemed human beings who will rule and reign with Christ: the Bride. The oldest Greek manuscripts of Revelation have the 24 elders referring to the redeemed as "them" and "they" (someone other than themselves). If this use of pronouns is accurate (and these are the pronouns found in the very oldest Greek manuscripts of Revelation which are closest to the time of its original writing), then the 24 elders would not be Bride members, and almost certainly not other human believers, which would mean they would have to be celestial beings.

BRO. T.G.: Bro. Baer, I have never heard it in that way. I'll have to study those points you made. Thank you.

BRO. W.M.: Cain murdered his brother Able, then God said to Cain: "What have you done? Listen! Your brother's blood cries out to me from the ground!" (**Genesis 4:10**). Even though a person can be dead, their blood can (figuratively) cry out. Blood is the evidence of the murder.

BRO. T.G.: Good scripture in Genesis, but very different than that in Revelation. I'm not sure how you understand the saints under the Old Covenant but I understand that no one could enter into the kingdom of heaven back there under the law. But, those Old Testament saints were looking for a promise, a kingdom whose builder and maker was God and not things that could be made with hands "here on earth". I saw this years ago, John the Baptist, Jesus Christ, the Apostles, and even the 70 who were sent out preached this message during the beginning of that early church reign. They all preached, "Repent ye for the kingdom of heaven is at hand".

So, we cannot compare that Old Testament scripture with what I used in Revelation. There was no life in the Old Testament. But the question is, When did the kingdom of God appear or come during that New Testament church period?

BRO. M.M.: I personally love this topic. It forces you to deal with things Christ said and to answer his questions. I see Bro. W.M. that you brushed off Bro. V.M.'s scripture and really didn't answer Christ's question.

I truly believe that Jesus laid the foundation to get us to perfection. All of his messages were how we should live. My pastor said over and over, "We teach the rule and work with the exception!" What does that mean? We continue to teach as Jesus did, to be perfect as his Father in heaven is perfect. Not everyone will comply to God's law. To say someone can't do this is odd to me. Why would Jesus teach us to do something that is out of reach for us working and with him leading? You are correct. It is not for us to say who has or hasn't reached any level in God. God is the judge of all. Again, in Revelation Jesus spoke to the churches and said, "to him that overcometh". Why would he make these statements? You might say, "Well it's not for us now, only back then or maybe it's yet to come". That's not our call. People also say that about the Holy Ghost, and we know that's not true. So, instead of looking for ways to make Jesus' question false, building doctrines that contradict his teaching, consider that anything he said is correct and we need to adjust our thinking. I hope you will consider the spirit I am making these statements in. I'm only saying this out of love for the truth and you.

BRO. BAER: Though I don't have sufficient time to clarify all the details of what I believe about this subject at the moment, maybe I'll just toss out some various thoughts on this topic for discussion. I think the principal issue that might divide us on this is related to defining what is meant by life and death in some of the statements used in the Bible. Both life and death can refer to a range of things, from being physically alive or dead to being spiritually alive or dead. What it means to be "alive to God" is another critical thing we have to properly define. Can someone be "alive to God" (not "dead" to Him) and yet still be physically dead: body and soul for those who differentiate the soul as something which can be separated from the body, which I do not. I believe there is *no* living soul except as part of a body. Adam was not a living soul *until* God's breath breathed into the vessel of his physical body. God didn't take a soul and put it in a body, He took a body and made Adam a living soul.

But, back to the issue of being "alive to God". Does the Bible teach that someone can be thought of as "alive" even if they are not actually alive as a body/soul anywhere? Does the Bible ever refer to the soul being alive after death? Not just to a person being considered "alive to God", but an actual statement that uses the words for soul (*nephesh* in the Hebrew or *psyche* in the Greek) and that states that someone's soul left their body or would leave their body? Just a few things to consider and discuss.

BRO. T.G.: Would third heaven angels be in the same category as we humans are? They never had to be redeemed as far as being saved from the curse of sin. So, why would this phrase in **Revelation 22:9** state that they keep the sayings of this book?

BRO. BAER: That is part of what I referred to regarding the Greek grammar of the passage (which may not have been clear on my part). The Greek wording and grammar that underlies that translation does not appear to be referring to this angel as one of the brethren who keep the sayings of the book. The way the *King James Version* translators translated it just makes it sound like that is what it is saying. It actually says that this angel is a fellow servant *like* John and his (John's) human brethren who keep the sayings of the book. In other words, what this actually says in the original language is that they are the same in terms of being servants of God, but it does not actually say that the angel is one of "thy brethren the prophets...which keep the sayings of the book". He is actually saying that he and they both are servants, but not that he and they (both) are prophets or that he and they (both) keep the sayings of the book.

The point is that in the original language of the Scripture, these passages actually may not be stating that this angel is one of them (as the English translation makes it sound), but only that he is similar to them in terms of being a servant. The rest of the description (according to the Greek grammar of the passage) is only meant to refer to them (and not to the angel). In **Revelation 5**, when the four beasts and 24 elders are speaking and praising God, it is a similar issue. The actual Greek wording of all of the oldest manuscripts of **Revelation 5** uses pronouns that express that the beast and elders were not among the redeemed, but were actually referring to the redeemed as individuals other than themselves: using pronouns like "they" to refer to "them" rather than the "we" and "us" that are used in the English translation of the *King James Version* (but which are not used in the oldest manuscripts of Revelation: those closest to the original writing of the book).

These three passages are the only passages in Revelation that seem to testify to the possibility that human beings might be in heaven prior to the Marriage Supper of the Lamb. But, if the preceding is correct (which it appears that it would have to be based on what the original language actually appears to say), then actually there would not be any statement in Revelation that supports that belief other than the souls under the altar in **Revelation 6**. But, those souls crying out are (to me) an entirely different issue. The description of them crying out (as if consciously alive somewhere) is exactly the same kind of language, and even the same type of context, regarding Abel's blood crying out (for justice) when Abel himself was clearly not alive or conscious anywhere at the time. He was alive in God's mind though, and that seems to be the point about his blood crying out: that God was aware of what had occurred, had not forgotten, and was moved to carry out justice for his murder.

BRO. T.G.: So, is our eternal hope any greater than those from the Old Testament as far as reaching that goal now, and looking for that great reward of the possibility of moving straight into eternal life if we complete the end of our salvation now? I mean what is greater (about the New Covenant faith) than what they had to look forward to under the Old Covenant? They were looking for the promise, a city, a resurrection, to live again. As Bro. C.P. stated, which is not word for word, "high balling the graveyard". I'm reminded by what Jesus said, "Fear not Him which is able to destroy (kill) the body but fear Him who is able to destroy by soul and body in hell" (**Matthew 10:28**). Jesus also said, "I am the resurrection if ye believe in me ye shall never die" (**John 11:25-26**). Paul stated that he knew a man above fourteen years ago who went somewhere, got a taste of something beyond this natural world into a realm that I wish to attain to also.

I'm not sure why this is not expressed more thoroughly in scripture by the Lord.. it seems there are only hints. Maybe more is given by being in the Spirit of the living God through revelation… that hidden manna. But, even the apostle Paul received things that he could not utter, like other prophets or angels in Revelation and the Old Testament like Ezekiel, Isaiah, or Job. Very interesting discussion.

BRO. BAER: It isn't my intent to contravene any teaching anyone has received on this subject from men of God they have sat under or have been influenced by. In my case, I was brought up with a strong tradition of teaching on the hope of the resurrection of the dead being a future, physical resurrection that is the product of a spiritual resurrection through the ongoing work of being spiritually "revived" as more and more of the old man dies and the new man is enlivened. All of us are the products of what we have been taught (at least to some degree, unless we have completely rejected all that we have been taught of course), and I am no different. I think it would be interesting to discuss the pros and cons of the variant views of this and the different biblical reasons for each.

Briefly (if such a thing is possible), I believe one of the major differences between the hope of the resurrection in the Old Testament and that in the New Testament is the inclusion of the possibility of being a part of the *first* resurrection: the opportunity not only to be in the Bride of Christ (as part of those who will rule and reign with Christ) but also the fact that those who rise in the first resurrection (which we see as a physical resurrection that is the product of a spiritual "resurrection") will be guaranteed eternal life and immortality and (as we have all commonly believed) a celestial (versus eternal terrestrial) body. This is why I believe Paul said what he did in his statement in **Philippians 3**.

Philippians 3:11-14 *If by any means I might attain unto the resurrection of the dead. Not as though I had already attained, either were already perfect: but I follow after, if that I may apprehend that for which also I am apprehended of Christ Jesus. Brethren, I count not myself to have apprehended: but this one thing I do, forgetting those things which are behind, and reaching forth unto those things which are before, I press toward the mark for the prize of the high calling of God in Christ Jesus.*

I believe Paul knew he would have had a resurrection under the Old Covenant and by faith in Christ, one under the New Covenant, but the New Covenant had opened up the possibility for a higher calling and a greater prize: the first resurrection and Bride membership.

I do believe that the details of the nature of the resurrection and the transition from one form to another, and/or from mortality to immortality is (as I think you alluded to) only spoken of very briefly and indirectly in the Scripture. There are passages that *might* refer to the idea of leaving the body at death (though that is not what I personally believe they communicate), and passages that might prove that a future physical resurrection is what is required. But, most of the processes (and even to some degree the timing) are veiled in mysterious language that could be taken several ways. One thing that I do know is that our experience of the transition would likely be the same either way, so as far as what we will undergo, it is unlikely to matter. If we immediately "move out" into a celestial body when our physical body dies, or if we rest in the hope of a future physical resurrection (though still "alive" to God: alive in His mind and memory), it will essentially be the same experience to us either way. In either case, we will almost certainly not experience any passing of time. We will close our eyes in death and open them again in the resurrection in what will be experienced by us as only a moment of time. For that reason, I don't feel any great anxiety regarding the differences we may have on some of the particulars. The experiential result (for us) will be the same regardless.

One point I will raise is the issue of the immortality of the soul versus the resurrection related to Paul's preaching on Mar's Hill in **Acts 17**. The Greeks believed in the immortality of the soul and wouldn't have been at all put off or surprised by Paul telling them they could "move out a live soul". But, when Paul talked to them about the resurrection of the dead (all the details of which don't appear to have been recorded) they laughed and mocked him. That would seem to imply that he was teaching something other than a soul living beyond the body, as they nearly universally believed that already.

There are several questions I might ask related to this: Was Lazarus alive somewhere in some form during the approximately four days his body lay dead in the tomb? Did Jesus say that Lazarus was dead? Did Jesus also say that Lazarus was asleep? Did that mean the same thing, or did he possibly have a deeper meaning behind in referring to him as sleeping when he clearly told the disciples that he was dead? Can a person who is actually truly dead (physically and otherwise) be still considered "alive" to God if they are "alive" in His mind and memory and if He intends to raise them back to conscious life?

BRO. T.G.: We do see eternal life (or immortality) could not yet be obtained at the time of Lazarus' death because Jesus had not yet completed his work here on earth. That was the door or entrance back into the kingdom Adam sold us out of.

BRO. BAER: Forgive me Bro. G., I didn't mean to refer to Lazarus as an example of someone who would or wouldn't have moved out as a live soul. My meaning in mentioning him was more related to the language Jesus used regarding him after he died. He referred to him from his (Jesus') perspective as if he was still alive, but just "sleeping". He did the same with the little girl he raised from the dead, and it seems clear that both were truly and fully dead and not alive somewhere else. My point is that when God and Christ (who have the power to resurrect an individual back to life) refer to the dead, who are *not* alive and conscious somewhere after their death, they do use language that sounds like they are saying that they are still alive somewhere when what they actually appear to mean is that from their perspective (being able to return them to life), they are only "sleeping". Thus, fully dead individuals could be considered still "alive" to God if He intends to "wake" them at some point and return them to conscious life. They are "alive" in His mind and still "alive" in the sense (poetically speaking) that He intends to return them to life.

On the other hand, those who will never receive a resurrection and be alive (again) are truly "dead" to God. This is at the heart of how we differentiate between being spiritually alive and being physically alive (including at the soul level). If someone is spiritually "alive to God" then, even if they are truly and fully physically dead, (body and soul) they will still have a resurrection. If someone is spiritually "dead to God", they will not have a future resurrection. Thus, the idea of someone being "alive to God" (from our perspective) is that they are "alive to God" (in His mind) and given that, they will receive a resurrection. He is presently calling those things that are not as though they are (**Romans 4:17**). They are not actually physically alive (body or soul), but He is calling them as such, and His promises refer to them as such because they are still alive to Him (in His mind and memory), and they will be alive when He calls them back into existence.

BRO. T.G.: Yes sir. Same understanding!

BRO. BAER: Romans 4:17 *(As it is written, I have made thee a father of many nations,) before him whom he believed, even God, who quickeneth the dead, and calleth those things which be not as though they were.*

God quickens the dead (brings them to life even *after* they are dead) and calls those things which be not (not alive) as though they are (alive). This seems to imply that God (and Christ in his statements as well) can refer to someone as being "alive", not because they are conscious somewhere, but because they are "alive to God". The context of this statement is the "dead" womb of Sarah, and even by extension the possible death of Isaac (if Abraham had sacrificed him at Mount Moriah). This last is inferred by the parallel statement in **Hebrews 11:19**.

Hebrews 11:19 *Accounting that God was able to raise him (Isaac) up, even from the dead (if Abraham had killed him); from whence also he received him in a figure.*

BRO. T.G.: Amen. God sees things totally different than we understand things.

BRO. BAER: That is how I believe His words are meant when it comes to the promise of eternal life. If we are truly His, even if we die (body and soul), we will still be alive to Him (in His mind and memory) and guaranteed by Him to resurrect to life in the future.

I know that sounds more complicated than simply saying that His words mean that they would never die at all (but their soul would continue living), but the claim that their soul would live on appears to directly contradict the biblical description of the soul and the entire message of the hope of the resurrection. That message was strange and new to that present world (of the Greeks and Romans especially) who already believed in the immortality of the soul (as attested to by history, **Acts 17**, etc.). The resurrection of the dead was a new message that was different than what they had believed. For that reason (and a number of others), I do not believe Paul was preaching the immortality of the soul (which is what moving out a live soul is... just a more selective version of it).

This is one of several reasons why I do not think that the meaning of Jesus's statements about believing in him means that belief would prevent anyone from ever truly dying (body and soul). I believe that what it meant was that you would not face eternal death: you will not be dead to God and facing a death from which this is no resurrection. Thus, it could simply mean that you will still be "alive to God" and you will not die without the hope of a resurrection (life). If it could be argued that his statements mean that those who believe in him will never die (in any true sense), that begs several very serious questions: Is only believing in him fully sufficient to merit an individual eternal life and immortality, or are there relational requirements that must be met as part of that belief / faith that includes obedience and spiritual maturation?

If we are basing our theology on a few selectively chosen passages that essentially say "Whosoever believeth in him should not perish, but have everlasting life" (**John 3:16**), what about the wording of **John 11:26**, where he said, "whosoever *liveth and believeth in me* shall never die"? Or, **Romans 8:13**, where Paul said, "For if ye live after the flesh, ye shall die: but *if ye through the Spirit do mortify the deeds of the body, ye shall live*"? What if you believe in him but still continue living after the flesh? I know that most of us realize that eternal life requires more than just belief, but there is a reason I am quoting these passages. Each of them (and others as well) demonstrate that there is more to receiving eternal life than just belief alone, and if that is so, then might it not be possible that the way we are quoting these (as proof someone who believes will receive eternal life without ever dying) might also be more layered as well?

BRO. T.G.: Amen, amen, and amen. There is a qualifying of our love to Him. For if we love Him we shall keep His commandments, maintain good works, cleanse ourselves from all filthiness of the flesh and spirit so that we can present ourselves holy and acceptable to God which is our reasonable service, that we may prove that good, acceptable, and perfect will of God in our own lives or in our own faith! Good discussion.

Just to clarify, I do believe that this earthly body will go back to the ground but I feel to lean more on we have a greater hope or reward than what the Old Testament saints were waiting on. I see that those Old Testament worthies in **Hebrews 11** came up in **Matthew 27:52**, resurrected into another body, received that promise which was the Spirit baptizing them, their entrance into that new kingdom, the kingdom of heaven, that earnest of their inheritance. I always wondered if they proved themselves faithful already before God in their day? Was all they were needing is the baptism of the Holy Ghost? What happened to those that continued on and reached that same place the apostle Paul eluded to in the book of Timothy, where he fought a good fight, kept the faith, and now there was a crown of righteousness awaiting him! I feel that crown of righteousness was a "new body", a celestial body not made with hands by mother and father but from God Himself. In other words, Paul possibly moved out and into his new house.

BRO. BAER: I think one of those greater rewards is the hope of the first resurrection, which (though I see as a resurrection of both body and soul) is a resurrection to unqualified, guaranteed eternal life and immortality (dramatically different from how nearly all of us believe the second resurrection to be). In addition, it is the right to rule and reign with Christ. And, the Holy Spirit within (under the New Covenant) allows for a far greater range of possible relationship with God than ever possible under the Old Covenant, meaning that even if someone comes up in the second resurrection, they would (potentially) be far further along the path necessary for entering into eternal life and immortality.

BRO. R.A.: This topic is of great interest to me. I believe the reason for contention on it among us is that if someone says they do not believe in moving out a live soul, this is taken to mean that one cannot attain to the Bride right now (yet). For many, saying you cannot make the Bride right now is anathema. I do believe there is a middle ground, being that the vast majority of Bride members will be produced in the early and latter rain church periods, but if someone can attain to that mark outside of those timeframes, that is completely in God's purview. It very well is possible someone could make it at any time, and it is probably best to leave that up to the Almighty. I believe the middle ground is that someone can attain to the Bride at any time. It is possible, but nobody is moving out anywhere, a resurrection will await.

I have heard that Jesus brought something far greater than "just" a resurrection. I would concur. Jesus brought in the ability to go on to absolute and full perfection. To say that Jesus brought in something greater and then leap to that meaning a Bride member goes straight to heaven and under the altar is a leap. That being said, with this issue, whether anyone moves out or not, whether it's instantly after death or hundreds of years, as far as we are concerned, our next conscious moment we will be with the Lord.

I think with lots of these finer details there simply is going to be a great variety of belief that likely will not be resolved until the restoration of the church. Whether it's the Devil, moving out a live soul, resurrections, etc., some of these topics have literally been debated for decades with no settled movement either way. These issues have been debated by sincere and godly men on either side. We have so much unity on our core beliefs, that there will be a Bride, that God is going to restore His church, our belief on the Godhead, eternal judgment, etc. These are items that Christendom sees vastly differently, but that we are by and large unified on. That doesn't mean we can't work on things, but to focus on what brings us together is a very healthy discussion. Jesus will have a church that will make up his bride, and it will be without spot or wrinkle or any such thing, but holy and without blemish!

BRO. BAER: Amen. Good thoughts. To wrap up some of this, the distinction we might think is being blurred by the belief in moving out a live soul is the distinction between the belief in the immortality of the soul, which was never taught or even inferred in the Scripture prior to Jesus's statements some believe are promising that hope and the physical resurrection of the dead. The preaching of the Gospel was the hope of the resurrection of the dead in contrast to the prevalent pagan belief in the immortality of the soul. Interpreting Jesus' statements to mean that he suddenly began teaching the immortality of the soul (for all people or just for Bride members) when there was no previous biblical basis of any kind for that belief is what I see as the problem. I think it is more likely that his statements about receiving eternal life are deeper in meaning than just belief equals moving out a live soul at death. The clear and consistent message of the Scripture is that of the hope of a full resurrection (body and soul) in the future rather than the immortality of the soul in the present. Outside of Jesus' statements in the Gospels, there are only a handful of passages in the entire New Testament that might infer (depending on how someone interprets them) the idea of moving out a live soul, and I believe they can be more easily explained with other interpretations.

I do think it is very likely that Jesus' statement are deeper in meaning, and rather than being a promise that no one who believes in him would ever experience death, they are a promise that no one who believes in him will ever experience eternal death: the second death. The idea that his statements on that issue are deeper than they sound on the surface is further reinforced by the fact that we know he could not have simply meant the surface level statement that "belief = guaranteed eternal life" as other statements he makes (and others do as well) proves that it is not merely belief that gives life, but "living and believing" in him, obeying his commandments, being holy and righteous, etc. Thus, the surface level (and potentially overly simplistic) reading and understanding of his statements, only some of which say that "he that believeth in him shall have eternal life", have to be deeper and fuller in meaning than can be understood just by cherry-picking them out without comparing them with the many others that appear to convey a very different idea.

ARI'EL INSTITUTE

ENCOUNTERS WITH EVIL SPIRITS AND OTHER SUPERNATURAL ACTIVITY

BRO. A.M.: Bro. Baer, I know personal experience never trumps scripture. That said, what are your thoughts on what people call ghosts? I have had several experiences with things that were certainly not the flesh and I'm pretty sure it wasn't an angel either. Have you had an experience like that or do you know someone who has?

BRO. BAER: If we're talking about spirit beings who appear to be evil, then I have had a number of experiences as well. There is no doubt that they were not righteous angels or celestial beings as the feeling of evil associated with them was palpable, and often their purpose was evil as well (to lead away from God, to bring confusion, to bring fear, etc.). What appears to be the most obvious interpretation of Scripture (especially in the Gospels when Jesus is dealing with evil spirits / devils) coupled with the many things I, and many others, have personally experienced seems to be overwhelming evidence of their reality (as something outside of ourselves). No one who has experienced such a thing in a lucid state would believe it is a figment of someone's imagination or just a mental condition, especially if some supernatural occurrence was associated with that experience (hearing a voice, seeing something, physical activity beyond human ability, etc.). In addition, I have experienced some of these things (very distinctively supernatural activity) in the presence of multiple others who also experienced them as well, which would be nearly impossible if it was merely one person's mental or emotional conditions (as I have sometimes heard some claim). There are certainly many folks who do struggle with mental and emotional conditions, and it is possible that their conditions may be confused with the work of evil spirits in some cases, but that fact is not sufficient to explain away the reality of evil spirits / devils in the Scripture or the type of experiences I am referring to.

BRO. V.M.: How do you know it wasn't an angel?

BRO. A.M.: I would think an angel would be around for a message, correction, protection, or punishment. This thing did none of those. Its purpose was purely just to make us afraid.

BRO. V.M.: Not necessarily. Fear is not an unusual reaction to angels. You would not necessarily know its purpose either. I had a similar experience. I have never been more afraid in my life.

BRO. M.L. (South Africa): Yes, but why would an angel make me afraid for no reason? After the fear, no word, no message, just nothing! Not even telling me not to be afraid but seemingly enjoying the fear I have? Are you saying God's good angels do that?

BRO. V.M.: Do you know they do not?

Hebrews 13:2 *Be not forgetful to entertain strangers: for thereby some have entertained angels unawares.*

BRO. BAER: Bro. M., the "strangers" in **Hebrews 13:2** are simply that: someone a person doesn't know but who they were (in that society) expected to show hospitality towards. Paul appears to be pointing out that an angel might appear as a human being (as they a number of times in the Scripture) and interact with someone who did not know they were an angel (which also happened in the Scripture several times). That would not be the same thing as a spirit being interacting with someone in such a way as to inspire terror or influence evil thoughts and feelings.

BRO. V.M.: No Bro. M.L., angels are not evil spirits.

Bro. Baer, I was only pointing out that you would not necessarily know you were in the presence of a spiritual being nor would you necessarily know its ultimate purpose in meeting with you or necessarily whether it meant good or evil.

BRO. BAER: I agree...that you would not know you are in the presence of a spiritual being. But, that type of encounter appears to be one in which you thought they were just a human being (a human "stranger") and thus it would not be the same at all to what we have been referring to as something supernatural changing the atmosphere around you. The point of **Hebrews 13:2** saying that they entertained angels "unawares" is that they had no idea they were dealing with celestial beings because they thought they were human beings. What we are referring to is exactly the opposite. We are certain we are not dealing with mere human beings, and in many cases, there is no being that is even visible, so it certainly couldn't be mistaken for a human being.

I do understand your point. But, a clear and unquestionable feeling of moral evil and malice is entirely different than how a righteous angel's presence feels. By moral evil, I am talking about something that God, or any righteous angel, would never convey. By malice, I am not just talking about fear based on the fact that something you are encountering is "other", "powerful", "supernatural", etc., I am talking about an awareness, not only that something is present that may do you harm, but that it would take pleasure in doing so. Again, unless we are talking about a very wicked human being who God is sending an angel to bring judgement upon, this is simply not the type of feeling that we would associate with a righteous angel, especially if the person feeling this malice and moral evil is trying to resist it and to do what is right.

God does not attempt to subvert us (entrap us) into doing moral evil:

Lamentations 3:36 *To subvert a man in his cause, the Lord approveth not.*

The Hebrew word ***avath***, translated "subvert" here means to "pervert" or to "make crooked". Many of the experiences we have been mentioning are examples of just that: the presence of a being that is attempting to subvert, pervert, or make crooked. Anyone experiencing these things recognizes clearly that they are (at least in part) an attempt to influence their thinking and actions to cause them to reject God, to reject His will, His purpose, or even His existence. God is not the author of that kind of influence. If He were, He would be doing exactly what this verse says that He does not approve of: entrapping us into doing evil, or at the very least, subverting us from serving Him. God does not approve of subverting a man from his cause (of trying to do the right thing), though He obviously does move to subvert men from doing the wrong things.

So, if a spirit being attempts to subvert a man from believing in or doing the right things when that man truly desires to believe and to do the right things, that spirit being cannot have been directed to do so by God. That means that if we see any spirit being doing so, it must itself be morally perverted.

God does permit evil spirits (the lying spirit of **1 Kings 22** for example) to influence and affect wicked men who are under His judgement, but He does not send nor would He allow a righteous angel to try to turn good men from their righteousness. The whole idea of a righteous angel trying to turn men from righteousness is incomprehensible. It would be entirely against the nature of a righteous angel to try to turn a righteous man (or at least one genuinely desiring to be righteous) to unrighteousness. Simple logic and biblically consistent interpretation demand that this type of action would be the work of an unrighteous (evil) angel or spirit being, which is exactly what we see in **1 Kings 22** and elsewhere.

As to your earlier question, "How do we know it wasn't an angel"?... I didn't say that it wasn't an angel. I just said it wasn't a righteous angel, as its communication and interaction was clearly intended to bring evil thoughts and actions, and to lead away from God, and when resisted in the Spirit and name of Christ, it desisted. That type of interaction would be insensible for a "good" angel. Regardless, it was a spirit being of some kind whatever classification we might put upon it.

BRO. V.M.: Many times, angels from God struck abject fear in those they came to. Why wouldn't a "good" angel obey if you resist it in the name of Christ also?

BRO. BAER: I didn't just refer to fear. I have been in the presence of a righteous angel that struck fear in me, but that presence did not bring a feeling of evil and darkness with it.

Why would you resist a good angel in the name of Christ? What would a good angel be doing that would require Christ's authority being called on to change its actions?

BRO. V.M.: If you didn't know what it was. I had such an experience. Angels in scripture have struck fear in people. I don't think you would know what kind of presence it is. I commanded it to depart in the name of the Lord and it did, but that doesn't mean it was evil.

BRO. BAER: I know the difference between a good feeling and an evil one my friend (not just fear or trepidation, but malice and dark thoughts). Why would a good angel be doing anything that would require you to command it to depart in the name of the Lord?

BRO. V.M.: Simply fear… which is common with angels.

BRO. T.G.: Then would not God's children just be void of judgment? I believe clearly the scriptures tell us that His word and the Holy Ghost should be able to teach us to discern between good and evil, to choose righteousness over unrighteousness, to walk in the light and not darkness, to choose the Spirit over the flesh, and to choose the church over the world. If the Holy Ghost would not teach us these things, we would be of all men most miserable, and confused.

BRO. BAER: No, Bro. M., fear of something is not synonymous with a feeling of evil and wickedness. We all have been in environments (I would imagine) where a feeling of evil was palpable (a place where terrible wickedness was occurring or had occurred). That feeling, if you have felt it, is nothing like the fear associated with a godly supernatural being appearing.

BRO. V.M.: I disagree, fear is fear.

BRO. BAER: Fear is only one of the feelings associated with these types of experiences. And, it is an oversimplification of the nature of fear to say, "fear is fear". Fear of something more powerful (or other) than you that is good is entirely different than fear of something that is evil. A feeling of being in the presence of something evil (and the many different ways that can manifest) is something very different from the feeling of being in the presence of something that is more powerful, but not malignant in nature. I have (as most of us have) been in the presence of other human beings bent on doing some terrible evil, or deeply perverted by sin in their thinking and feelings. I may have had no personal fear of them, but the feeling of "darkness", perversion, malice, etc. was tangible in their presence. It may not have been aimed at me personally, and I may have felt no fear, either due to that fact or to the fact that I was in no way intimidated by them, but I did feel a tangible evil around them. The fact that I was not intimidated by them nullifies confusing that feeling with personal fear, which is exactly what it would be if we are talking about a "good" angel: fear based on intimidation or respect. Neither intimidation nor respect were involved. It was simply a tangible feeling of evil... and that is exactly the feeling when I have encountered this type of supernatural presence. Fear may have been involved, but it also included a consciousness of being in the presence of evil. Not just "evil" in the sense of something "bad" that might happen (to me, if I was not right with God, and this was a righteous angel), but moral perversity and spiritual darkness. Fear might (at least in part) be motivated by that awareness, but it was the product of it, and not confused with it.

I have been in the presence of a "good" angel, and there is a very distinct difference between the feeling of being so and what I just described. I was rescued from drowning by one as a child, and several other individuals were present and witnessed the event as well. There was a fear (that was based on a number of factors), but it was nothing like the fear *and* feeling of evil and moral perversity that could be felt in the other, opposite types of experiences. The entities were different in every way. The only similarity of feeling in their presence being an "otherness" that could generate fear regardless of whether they were good or evil. But, there was a dramatically different feeling of one versus the other. The first was like being in the presence of a benevolent, but powerful authority figure. The second was like being in the presence of a serial killer.

BRO. V.M.: I have never been afraid of something I believed meant good or no harm to me. If you do not realize it means no harm or even what it is you might feel fear. I have never experienced a presence anything like it before or since, the fear of the unknown would overrule any logic. It is human nature. Scripture teaches that sometimes angels struck fear into the hearts of people so much so that they feared for their lives. That is fear.

BRO. BAER: "Afraid" is a tricky word as sometimes "fear" (at least in the Bible) is meant to convey a feeling associated with the recognition of a power and authority far beyond our own (as in the case of the fear of the Lord). At other times it is intended to convey a feeling of dread and trepidation. Context and condition would determine which is being referred to. I agree with you that an encounter with the unknown and something "other" can produce the kind of fear you are referring to, though that is not the feeling I am talking about. I am talking about a feeling of evil and personal malice that is nothing like simple fear of the unknown, of something supernatural, or of something so powerful or different that it is "frightening". Those are (at least to someone who has experienced both... and I have) very different feelings.

The problem (if you can call it that) is that you cannot accept that any spirit being or angel could intend moral evil, or at least not as part of its own nature. Thus, you have to keep coming back to the feeling that those of us have experienced, in what we are certain were interactions with an evil spirit being, being just fear of a good spirit being. Fear is not the issue; a feeling of moral depravity and wickedness is. You may want to try to shift the focus to the feelings we have felt when encountering a spirit being of this kind to just being the product of fear, but that is simply not possible. It is not fear of the unknown or "other" that is the only thing that was present in these encounters, it was a tangible consciousness of the presence of something evil. Since you are unable (or unwilling) to comprehend of an evil spirit being you are just trying to redefine our experience of encountering something terribly evil as our apparent (fairly ignorant if it were) mistaking "other" for "evil". I'm sorry, but that is simply not possible, no matter how much your presuppositions about angelic beings and spirits demand (for you) that it must be. We have experienced something (and there are a very large number of folks who have throughout all of history) that is not only supernaturally "other", but which is supernaturally evil. That only leaves you with two choices. You either have to assume that all of the many millions of individuals who have had such experiences throughout history are mentally ill (including me, and many ministers and saints among our body of churches), regardless of how rational and emotionally balanced we have demonstrated ourselves to be, or you are going to have to admit that there is supernatural activity that you have either not experienced, or that you have blinded yourself to by your doctrinal biases. Are you truly going to make the argument, after interacting with so many of us who have had these types of experiences, that everyone who believes other than the way you do about evil spirits is mentally deranged and only those who believe as you do are not? You might want to consider that a bit more carefully.

BRO. A.M.: The fear I have felt while in the presence of evil spirits was almost always accompanied with a thought that nothing (including God) could make me safe. I have seen an angelic being one time (that I know of) and due to previous experiences, I wasn't afraid. I was grateful for the protection. The fear one feels when in the presence of evil spirits is an almost irrational, isolating fear. From what I can tell it appears to be aimed at terrorizing and causing doubt. We do see fear of angels in the Bible, but it almost always comes with the recognition of uncleanness of humanity in their presence. Men recognized their failings and admitted they were worthy of death, as was the case of Isaiah in his vision, or the parents of Samson. Samson's parents were interesting though because until the angel touched the rock with his staff and caught the sacrifice on fire, they thought they were talking to a normal man.

BRO. BAER: Bro. M., our experiences are very similar. I don't want to follow up your experiences by always giving another of my own (as yours are require no addition), but I feel like I have to add this one after what you said. When I was younger (in my teens) I woke up one night (I was alone in the house) with a feeling of terrible evil present. All of the lights were out and I got out of bed and walked to the top of the stairs. I could tangibly feel someone was in the house. We had a landing halfway down the stairs, and when I got to the top of the stairs, I turned on the light over the stairs. A man was standing on the landing (halfway up) looking up at me with the most evil expression of malice, blended with a look of almost mocking sarcasm (I don't have the words to describe it, but it was one of the most terrible combination of things I have ever seen in an individual's expression). A feeling just like you described washed over me, and a strong certainty that there was no God or any other being that could deliver me from this individual struck me, so powerfully it almost felt like my heart would stop. And, by the way, at that point in my life I was a very tough and hardened individual living in the midst of gangs, constant danger, etc. and somewhat inured to feeling much fear. I knew without the slightest doubt that this individual was the source of this feeling: like he was sending it to me, putting it in my mind. The stronger it came over me, the more that his mocking, sardonic, arrogant smile widened. I closed my eyes and cried out to God for help (despite the fact that I wasn't in a right relationship with Him at that time). When I opened my eyes again, the being was gone. I searched the entire house from top to bottom, and every door and window was locked from the inside.

Now, that was only one of several experiences I had with the very same being, and each experience included that nearly overwhelming pressure to reject God's reality and any relationship with Him. It was exactly the opposite of what God Himself would direct someone to experience. It was a feeling of undeniable evil and hatred of God and God's people. God delivered me from it, or I would not be here today... and no amount of argument could ever convince me it was not real. After all, a man with an experience is not at the mercy of mere arguments.

BRO. R.H.: I have heard somewhere that God lets those of us that are going to work casting out demons have these experiences so we will recognize that feeling. The man you saw was very tall I would guess. I have had some experiences with them, and they were not very pleasant experiences.

BRO. V.M.: 1 John 4:1 *Beloved, believe not every spirit, but try the spirits whether they are of God: because many false prophets are gone out into the world.*

BRO. BAER: Absolutely... and that would be true whether we are talking about "spirits" of men (the point of John's statement) or "spirits" in the unseen realm.

What makes this subject more complex for the interpretation of individual passages is that the words translated "spirit" or "Spirit" (**ruach** in Hebrew or **pneuma** in Greek) have a wide range of possible meanings that require comparison (with other passages), context, and grammar to aid in proper interpretation. As I know you know, these words can mean the "Spirit" of God (whether His power, presence, disposition, etc.), the "spirit / breath" of living things, the "spirit / disposition" of human beings, or even "wind" or "breath". And, we believe that they can also refer to "spirit" beings (celestial / spirit entities, angels, etc.). In the case of **1 John 4:1** the context seems to be a reference to human false prophets who have a carnal "spirit", though some might argue that, just like in the case of the lying spirit of **1 Kings 22**, there might be "spirit" beings instigating this false prophecy who themselves are revealed by the realization that these prophets are false and there are lying spirits behind their prophecies. Thus, it could be their own spirits that are causing them to prophesy falsely, or it could be the influence of spirit beings (like the lying spirit). I would have no problem seeing either possibility, as in my view both are possible sources for deception: being deceived by someone else (outside of yourself) or being self-deceived.

Though I am not making this case for **1 John 4:1** (which certainly might be intended as the "spirits" of men), when I come to passages that refer to spirits that also are called "devils" in the Greek, or in parallel passages (one Gospel calling them "spirits" and another "devils" for example) I know, based on the only possible meaning of the Greek words translated "devils" or "demons", that they can only be "spirit" beings. Those Greek words only mean spirit beings when used in that way, and have nothing to do with a person's disposition other than as an expression of how a spirit being is affecting them. There can definitely be a difference between someone who is "devilish" (acting like a "devil") and a "devil" who they are acting like.

BRO. V.M.: People feared they would die in the presence of God's angels. That is far from good or pleasant feelings. You cannot possibly know if a spirit means good or evil without it actually doing something.

BRO. BAER: Why would you believe that God would not allow someone to discern between good and evil spirit beings? If there are both (which there clearly are), then of course he would allow His people to discern the difference. God allows us to discern human beings in this way (**1 Kings 20:41**, etc.), so if there are spirit beings, why would that be any different? Given that there are both clean (righteous) and unclean (unrighteous) spirits and we are intended to be able to discern between things and individuals that are holy and profane, clean and unclean, righteous and unrighteous (**Ezekiel 44:23, Malachi 3:18**), this would seem to go without saying. In addition, statements like **1 Corinthians 12:10** referring to "discerning of spirits" is not qualified by the context as to what kind of spirits Paul is referring to and could certainly be saying that very thing: being able to discern between different (good or evil) spirits (spirit beings), just as easily as it could mean to discern between different spirits (dispositions) that human men might have.

You are either ignoring or just not hearing the numerous testimonies (quite a few given in these discussions of late) of folks who did not just feel a bad feeling (like impending judgement), but who felt something morally evil pulling them toward moral evil, toward rejecting God or even God's existence. The problem is that you continue misclassifying the feelings we are describing. We are not talking about simple dread or trepidation; we are talking about ***moral evil*** and ***an influencing pressure to reject God***. These are entirely different things. Your doctrinal biases are what are causing you to conflate these, or to persistently ignore the descriptions of these experiences since they don't fit with your predisposed "world view". Your presuppositions about what can and cannot be true regarding evil spirits (which are in no way based on any biblical evidence that requires or even clearly expresses your view… quite the opposite) force you to keep attacking a "straw man" you have made yourself. We are describing experiences that many thousands (if not millions) of people have had throughout history that include a darkness, moral depravity, and pressure to reject God and God's will that would never be feelings associated with a spirit that God had sent, and certainly are not descriptions of what someone would feel in the atmosphere if a holy angel were present. Once again, these experiences are not merely "fear" of something supernatural, they include an distinct awareness of something morally depraved, wicked, and malicious.

BRO. A.M.: Simple, it hasn't happened to him and hasn't been personally revealed to him. Therefore, it's not true.

BRO. BAER: As the old saying (that I referred to earlier, which is very pertinent to this discussion) goes: "A man with an experience is never at the mercy of a man with an argument". In the case of this subject, I believe I have a very strong argument for our belief based on far greater biblical and contextual consistency in our interpretation, the only proper use of grammar (of the biblical languages, and even in general), and a very strong and very large number of experiences (witnesses), some of which are far beyond the possibility of personal subjectivity since multiple other persons experienced them at the same time as well.

BRO. A.M., Bro. V.M., I am an ex Catholic. Catholicism is a religion steeped in error and traditions of men. I feel that God has blessed me with this contrast to his word so that I am especially skilled at exposing false doctrine and false traditions of men. When you are exposed to traditions of men masquerading as true worship you become jaded through pressures such as peer pressure to believe what your particular denomination or organization believes and teaches. There is also the powerful pressure of your own family and friends who will sway your thinking. Imagine a Catholic being taught that confessing to a priest will absolve them of any sin, and having been taught that for literally thousands of years, generation after generation. Taking someone like that to task in trying to help expose this false belief not only means they will have to accept that they are believing error but that their families and friends also are and those who have passed on before them, that they loved, died believing error. What a terrible pill to swallow. I am asking many of you to swallow a similar pill.

Mark 7:6-13 *He answered and said unto them, Well hath Esaias prophesied of you hypocrites, as it is written, This people honoureth me with their lips, but their heart is far from me. Howbeit in vain do they worship me, teaching for doctrines the commandments of men. For laying aside the commandment of God, ye hold the* *tradition of men, as the washing of pots and cups: and many other such like things ye do. And he said unto them, Full well ye reject the commandment of God, that ye may keep your own tradition. For Moses said, Honour thy father and thy mother; and, Whoso curseth father or mother, let him die the death: But ye say, If a man shall say to his father or mother, It is Corban, that is to say, a gift, by whatsoever thou mightest be profited by me; he shall be free. And ye suffer him no more to do ought for his father or his mother; Making the word of God of none effect through your tradition, which ye have delivered: and many such like things do ye.*

BRO. V.M.: My wife and I were visited by a spirit forty years ago and to this day we cannot tell you definitively if it was good or evil. You have no scripture for what you claim, and that's fine, as it doesn't seem to matter anyway, but please don't get upset with me if I call out fables.

BRO. BAER: No scripture? That is an incredible statement given the many scriptures in the Bible that describe evil spirits, devils, and demons (all of which appear to be referring to the same type of beings). We may have "no scriptures" that you can see, but there are many, many scriptures that are very clear to the majority of folks simply reading what the Bible simply says and who simply let the language say what it says without coloring it over with their own extra-biblical conceptions. I truly appreciate that you are willing to say that you were not sure whether the spirit you encountered was good or evil. We have to be careful not to be so hardline dogmatic on issues that are much broader and deeper than any of us may be capable of fully understanding.

BRO. R.H.: It is not a problem for those of us with the Holy Ghost who have worked at casting out demons to feel when one of them is present. As my first pastor used to say, when you talk about evil spirits don't get full of what you are discussing. I would like to keep the unity of the spirit in the bonds of peace until we get the truth on every subject. God Bless you my brother.

BRO. BAER: Well said Bro. H.

BRO. V.M.: You have never cast out a demon nor could you ever prove it. Fables like that give true believers a bad name. Next, you'll claim you or someone close has the gift of healing. I do not believe you.

BRO. BAER: Bro. M., those kinds of statements are the product of refusing to accept anyone's experiences other than your own, any history other than that which (supposedly) supports your preconceptions, and any scriptures that could contradict your claims. And, that type of blind dogmatism and stubborn refusal to accept anything (no matter the weight of evidence) that calls your spiritual worldview into question is the eventual product of arbitrary methods of interpretation (extreme over-allegorization of anything that doesn't fit your beliefs for example). This kind of blatant ignoring of evidence and experience is why you believe what you do. It is why I think that arbitrary forms of interpretation (for example, heavy allegorization of many clear statements of Scripture) is so potentially dangerous. It can lead to the kind of blind extremes that you hold. As to the spiritual realm, when someone reinterprets the words for "devils" into mental and emotional conditions, when those words ("devils" or "demons") always and only referred to spirit beings and the affects they caused in the *koine* Greek used in the New Testament, and when many other words could have been used for mental and emotional conditions (if that is what they were), they are allowing their own beliefs to change the meaning of what the Bible actually says and the only reasonable and biblically consistent definitions of words. This is because otherwise they will have to accept that their conclusions about the spirit realm (at least in part) have to be incorrect.

As relates to this issue, or to the issue of healings (which you also reject as real), there is no evidence (biblical, historical, or experiential) that will ever be good enough evidence for you to accept it as evidence. So, it might be best to stop claiming you have to have evidence (as you have asked for many times in these discussions) when there is no evidence, no matter how strong, that you would ever accept as actual evidence. I am sorry, and I wish it were not so, but you seem to have blinded yourself by your personal biases. One of your comments to another brother really stood out to me when you said something to the effect of "If my wife had been healed of an issue of blood after twelve years I would believe". You sound so like those who rejected Christ and his work in the New Testament that it is heart-rending. Why are *you* personally the only basis for these things being true? What if someone else said their wife was healed? Your wife being healed would prove it to *you*, but many others wives, husbands, children, friends, etc. of other people being healed is not good enough evidence? The only evidence that matters is based on your own experience and never on the experiences of anyone else? Whether you realize it or not, that statement says a great deal. And again, don't say that others don't have evidence, so they can't make that claim. As to healings, several told you (and I have given you similar evidence) that medical reports showed the condition was gone, and the person who knew it was healed and felt the Spirit **when** the healing took place. If you will not accept a Spirit-filled brother's testimony (and there have been many who have given you testimonies these last few weeks) that he felt the Spirit, and then the condition was gone, **_combined with_** the fact that a medical report showed that it was present previously and is now no longer present, you might want to just admit that no evidence, no matter how indisputable, will be something that you will allow to correct your claims or to reverse your position.

BRO. V.M.: Just because there *were* evil spirits and divine healing in the Scripture doesn't prove, two thousand years later, that there *are* now. Where multitudes were getting healed by gift, and Paul raised a man from the dead, very shortly after Paul had to leave a man who was a great help to him behind, sick. Worse than not having these gifts operating or seeing them sunset is to not have them yet be so convinced without evidence that you see them happening. That is a sad delusion indeed. You are of good company, as the assembly I came up in believes similarly, at least regarding divine healing, even in the face of sickness and death. So very frustrating to me to see Holy Ghost filled people believe and live fables.

BRO. A.M.: You remind me of someone I know. He didn't believe in speaking in tongues and claimed it had ceased with the apostles. A few months later he heard a noise coming from his bedroom. It was his wife. She was on the floor speaking in tongues. She couldn't even talk in English. He changed his doctrine that day. I hope you get an experience like that.

BRO. BAER: I pray the same. Bro. V.M., you can't just pick and choose what you personally believe is present and what is not. The very arguments you are using for the cessation of nearly all the order and activity that was present in the early church are the same ones that individuals make for arguing that the baptism of the Spirit is false. It would be more intellectually consistent for you to argue (God forbid) that the baptism of the Holy Spirit (and speaking in tongues in general) is no longer present, like you believe about spirits, healings, etc., as its presence is based on (in great part) some of the very same types of evidences you keep rejecting. Either the baptism of the Spirit *and* its associated operations (including healing) are present, or it is not. We simply believe that it is, and that they are.

Your cherry-picking of what you want to believe and not believe out of a package of beliefs and facts is beyond unreasonable. Your method of denying clear facts that don't support your conclusions only emphasizes that your beliefs are based on personal bias. Your rejection of all testimonies and experiences of everyone but yourself is not only heartbreaking, but it is highly disrespectful of those who are just as certain about their experiences as you appear to be that they are false. You are right my brother, it is sad. It is sad to see you so certain of your claims of uncertainty.

BRO. A.M.: I had an experience that stands out to me because it involved physical objects outside of my control and there were witnesses. My sister, my mother, and I were in a small country church practicing singing. We paused to change songs and I was sitting several pews away from the front to see what the sound was like. To my left was the dining room door. While they were paused the doorknob turned and then the door swung open. About ten seconds later a door just beside the platform opened and then closed. My mom grabbed her papers and said that we'll practice a different day. The dining room door was one of those doors that you have to push open because the frame was stuck. The weird thing about this is we all heard the knob jiggle and then we watched it turn. When it opened, we fully expected to see someone walk through. When the second door opened and closed by itself, we decided to leave. The odd thing is we didn't feel anything evil or fearful. At least not until we realized what had happened. I've since then felt and seen things like that in other places but there was an accompanying evil feeling.

BRO. BAER: I had a very similar experience once, with a door opening and closing that could not have done so by itself. In that case it was preceded by a feeling of something evil approaching, then three of us who were present all saw the door handle turn and the door open. It changed the atmosphere of the group very quickly, and all of us saw and felt it.

BRO. T.G.: When the Lord Jesus was calling me to salvation, in the night while I was asleep, I would wake up out of a dead sleep because I felt something watching me at my bedroom door. Several times this would happen. A few times, my bed would shake when I closed mine eyes and after opening them it would stop.

Then after I gave my life to Jesus, I witnessed a young man in the Baptist church that I attended somehow open himself up to demons that possessed him, and I heard voices screaming out of this young man, seemingly trying to invoke fear in me and deceive me into thinking it was of God. I can remember them saying, we have the faith of Meshach, Shadrach and Abednego.

Since after being saved, I have had temptations come to me in my dreams, and as I would try to awake, something would hold me, try to stop me from saying Jesus, again using fear as a tormentor.

I remember praying with some at the altar and in the person's eyes it was not them looking back at you but something else. After continually believing in the power of God and calling on the name of Jesus, that person "came to", and got some help from the Spirit of God. I believe these could be what the Bible calls "strongholds", or spiritual wickedness in high places: what Bro. Baer called evil angels.

BRO. D.P. (Canada): In a time of separation, and isolation from others and a wrong judgement against me, I felt hands come around my neck and choke me. When the word of God was uttered the choking left. The feeling was real and the deliverance was so liberating. God will stand with you. Just keep from evil and develop a discernment of evil and good.

BRO. BAER: I might point out that in nearly all of my personal experiences where I felt directly threatened or I felt an evil influence to do moral evil and/or to leave the Lord, were during the time when I was a young person who was out of church. I had left God's covering, and I believe He allowed me to experience some of those things as a direct result of withdrawing his barrier of protection. Though I do not want to initiate a discussion on the Devil right now, it is what I would consider being allowed to be turned over to Satan (at least to a degree). Now, before anyone might argue that God was personally directing these "evil" entities (rather than just permitting them) and/or that they were doing His will as "good" angels... in every case, there was a terrible feeling of *malice* (not just fear of harm due to judgement, but of someone who personally would take joy in hurting you) and *moral evil*. And, almost none of the experiences I had could possibly be described as things intended to draw me closer to God (to cause me to repent, return to relationship, etc.), scare me back on the right path, etc. Most of them involved an attempt to pull me away from God, from belief in Him, from the comfort of His presence, and to influence me to think or to do moral evil.

It is my personal belief (though, of course, based on Scripture as well) that God may permit (allow) evil spirits to act in ways that might seem detrimental (and they may even think what they are doing will be detrimental) when the end result may be to get His children's attention and cause them to realize what they are in danger of outside of a right relationship with Him, etc. On the other hand, I also think that He can allow (permit) a persistent condition, persecution, or oppression of some kind to occur like I believe He did with Paul in allowing the messenger of Satan to be present (in whatever way that it was) to keep Paul humble.

I have also experienced evil presences and manifestations when I *was* in a right relationship with the Lord (among His people, in church, etc.), though generally much less in occurrence and very different in feeling. Even when dealing with something very directly, it has felt as if a barrier was present between me and whoever or whatever was being affected, and though I could tangibly feel the evil present, I did not feel directly threatened or in any way fearful. As a pastor I have had to deal with a number of these types of conditions, and they have carried a very different feeling than when I was a young person outside of church.

BRO. A.M.: I have had those experience too. Once after coming back from a trip out of town, my wife was asleep in bed and I walked into my bedroom to go to bed as well. There was a white figure right beside my bed. It walked into my closet and disappeared. It didn't feel evil and I was tired, so I decided to just go to bed. When I got in bed my wife tapped my arm and asked why I was in the closet with the light on. I didn't want to spook her so I told her it wasn't me but don't worry about it. The next morning I told her what happened and she had seen it in the closet so I knew I wasn't crazy.

BRO. BAER: That sounds very like an experience my wife had. In the very early days of our pastoring here in Mansfield (about fifteen years ago) I was under a heavy emotional and spiritual load that was nearly beyond my ability to bear. One night after we had fallen asleep, my wife was awakened by a presence in the room. She sat straight up in bed (completely awake) and saw an angel standing over my side of the bed looking down on me with a look of deep compassion and protectiveness. It gave her such a feeling of peace that she just lay back down and went back to sleep, which I find astonishing, as I wouldn't have been able to resist the urge to interact. When she told me the experience in the morning, the feeling that came over me changed my entire state of mind for some time. The simple knowledge of what she had seen lifted the strain of the burdens I was under entirely. As a postscript, she is not a person who is given to these kinds of experiences (some folks who seem to always be having a new dream, experience, etc.). To my knowledge she has never seen an angel at any other time since.

BRO. A.M.: Same here. That's the one time I know I saw one. The contrast between the two is amazing (between the good and the evil).

BRO. BAER: Amen. The contrast is stark. These are not the same types of beings in terms of their moral state and motives.

Outside of the many (in my view) biblically clear and consistent evidences (Jesus talking to the evil spirits as if separate from the person who has them, casting them out into other places, creatures, etc.) and biblically linguistic evidences, such as spirits and devil (demons) referred to as synonymous, and the latter never used in *koine* Greek for anything other than spirit beings separate from human beings, etc.) that I personally believe demonstrate the existence of evil spirits as *more* than just mental and emotional conditions originating only within the minds of human beings. There is another more troubling issue that belief produces. If all evil spirits are only deranged mental and emotional issues the humans just *thinking* they are experiencing something (as some claim), and there are no actual external evil spirits who are spirit beings, then every single person (including many Spirit-filled believers and many ministers and saints in our body of churches) who have had experiences with evil spirits, that they are certain were spirit beings external to themselves, must either be classified as "liars" (they are making patently false claims) or "lunatics": they are all mentally or emotionally deranged by their own evil human spirit to the degree that they are completely certain that there was something tangibly present that was external to them when it was "all in their head", which would have to mean that they are all mentally ill. And, those who have not had these kinds of external experiences (of an evil spirit that is experienced as separate from themselves) must, by logical conclusion, be the only truly sane folks.

Do we really want to make that kind of claim that demands that kind of conclusion? Do we really intend to conclude that all of the many ministers and saints in our body (who I would imagine are presently much more than half of those in this body), and the many folks outside of our body of churches, who have had these kinds of experiences are all the victims of mental and emotional illness (insanity) while those who believe differently are the only ones not mentally or emotionally deranged? That is, whether folks realize it or not, the logical conclusion of the claim that all evil spirits are only the product of the person who thinks they are experiencing them being mentally or emotionally unstable, ill, or insane. If that is truly what someone believes, they will then have to classify all of those who do not agree with them (no matter that they are Spirit-filled, Spirit-anointed, clearly men and women of spiritual integrity, spiritual maturity, etc.) as being spiritually deranged while those who claim that no evil spirits exist are the only ones who are not. We need to think about the actual repercussions or our beliefs and how slanderous they may be of others who are no less sane or spiritually mature.

For this reason, and many others, it is my humble belief that we must be very careful not to make claims about what dogmatically has to be true without thinking through the full implications of our claims. It might sound reasonable (to someone who has not truly studied the Hebrew or Greek, the historical beliefs of the ancient Jews, or who has not had an experience of their own) to conclude that evil spirits are just human spirits, but it is not linguistically, contextually, historically, or experientially viable. Human beings can certainly have their evil spirits (dispositions), but claiming that all evil spirits are human not only is unviable in light of the actual terms and descriptions used for them, that belief demands the conclusion that all those who have experienced evil spirits are falsifying their experiences or are so mentally deranged that they cannot tell the difference between what is in their head and actually occurring around them (and sometimes occurring to others who are witnessing it simultaneously). Making that claim slanders the character and mental health of every man of God and saint that disagrees with it.

ARI'EL INSTITUTE

DOES GOD STILL HEAL TODAY?

EDITORIAL NOTE: The following was instigated by and part of the preceding discussion on supernatural activities and spirits, and became a separate discussion on its own

BRO. V.M.: In forty plus years of observation I have never once seen anyone possessed with an evil spirit or one cast out, although I have seen what I believe are unintentional fakes. Neither have I seen anyone divinely healed, although I have seen many unintentional fakes and simple wishful thinking. You can claim anything when no one asks you to prove it and almost everyone will believe it without question. No one can convince me God will heal one person's hemorrhoids but the blind, bedridden, cancer-filled, dying, and lame from birth go without (those for whom healing would be demonstrable and obvious). The God I know does not work that way and the Scripture bears me out. There is not one single case in the Scripture of God turning away someone who came for healing.

Two great apostles of God were in a serious disagreement involving doctrine that, on its face, could be argued wasn't of great importance. This incident teaches us that we must at times take a stand against what we see as an important principle even if it means strong criticism and friction. It may well be that if God entrusts you with truths that he expects you to teach them and stand up for them even in the face of resistance, shunning and criticism.

BRO. BAER: The last is true, but only true if you truly have been entrusted with the truths you are teaching. I would imagine most of us (if not all of us) would believe the same, which is why I often use the word "subjective" to refer to our beliefs that are just that. The fact that we (any of us) believe we have been given truths that are different from nearly anyone else's is dangerously subjective. The full package of what you believe (on healing, spirits, prophecy, the book of Revelation, etc.) that I am aware of (let alone things we haven't discussed) is different in that full package from any other person's teaching I know of. There are certainly those who believe pieces and parts of what I understand you to believe, but I have never met anyone else who believes the whole package of beliefs that you do (and I have met many, many thousands from a wide range of views). That uniqueness is either a glorious testimony to your special calling and anointing (which would obviously have to be in contrast to the rest of us, and most all other teachers as well) or, and I just want you to consider this, that though you may have some wonderful truths, and though I may be wrong on things you believe you are right on, the number of things you believe differently (and dramatically so) than everyone else may be a telling sign that not all that you hold so dogmatically as true is actually true. Gently said my brother. I have never been mad at you and never intended to be overly hard in any statements. I just want you to consider.

As to your comments on fakery going on in healings and spiritual manifestations, as well as in what is assumed to be the work of evil spirits... I agree. Of course there is fakery. There has always been. But, that does not preclude the reality of these things, it simply conveys that there is an orchestrated (in my view supernatural) effort to confuse and diminish the actual with a flood of the opposite. I have (and many, many others have as well) experienced *both* in all of the categories you mentioned. I have seen emotionalism disguised as the work of the Spirit and I have seen falsification of signs and wonders, as well as unconsciously or completely consciously (deliberate) "fake" healings. But, I have also seen the real thing, and not just a few times. I have also experienced the reality of spirit beings that could not be a figment of my imagination a number of times. Many others have as well. The fact that you claim you have not (at least as regards healings) is unfortunate, and the fact that you have seen fakery is simply par for the course, but neither of those claims can counter the many experiences that very many people *have* had. Your lack of experience cannot (and should not even be considered by you as able to) override the experiences of others.

BRO. V.M.: I have forty plus years of honest and unbiased observation of Holy Ghost people who I dearly love and care about but who are deluded by the teaching of deluded teachers. The teachers of these things will pay a greater price. Almost all manifestations so called of the Holy Ghost are not real even though manifested by mostly well-meaning people. That is my disturbing and unbelievable conclusion and I do not make it lightly nor am I anything but sorrowful about it.

BRO. BAER: Bro. M., on the issue of God being behind healings in this present day, not only do my own experiences (and those of many others) testify to that fact, but the Bible itself never states or infers that God would cease healing anyone after the time of the early church, or (as you seem to imply) that if He is not healing everything, He is not healing anything. Even in the days of the early church, there were only a handful of recorded resurrections of the dead out of what had to have been many thousands of Christians dying of old age, sickness, persecution, etc. It has never (*yet*) been God's methodology to have an "all or nothing" approach to healings. Even if you could argue that a number of *supposed* healings may not be coming from God in our day, that is not evidence that He is not still healing. Even if you could argue that it is mysterious and (to us) appears to be confusing that God would heal some things and never heal other things (suffered by those who are faithful saints), that is simply what we see all through the Bible, so it also isn't an evidence against His present healing. It is how He has always worked in the past. God never did heal everyone who we might think was deserving. He has always only healed at His own (mysterious) prerogative and with a selection process for doing so that is certainly not clear to us. That is nothing new, or just true of our day. It has always been the case.

If God is not healing and folks who are just recovering naturally are giving Him credit for their recovery, that is *far* less problematic than if He *is* healing and folks (like you) are claiming He is not, leading others to believe He is not, and by extension causing them not to thank Him for what He has done for them. I would be *far* more concerned with the possibility that He *is* working and we are denying His work (and not showing gratitude for it) than that, according to you, He is not responsible for the good things we are experiencing and it is, according to you, horrific that we would thank Him and credit Him for allowing good things (including healing, recovery, etc.) to occur. Even if He were not directly involved, His allowance of good things happening still should cause us to thank Him. If anything good happens to us, wouldn't that mean that God had to have, at the very least, allowed it to happen? If you simply think about this rationally, it is clear which would be worse, and if you are wrong, what you are teaching is *far* more devastating to the faith of the saints and to God's good name than if we are all wrong and we are thanking God for good things that He didn't provide.

BRO. V.M.: I have been thinking about this. If a person is raised in church to believe every time that they get sick they must pray for healing because, of course, God heals, because He is a healing God. Of course, most of the time they recover from relatively common sickness and disease. They thank God and testify of their healing, never mind those who do not receive healing. That just must be God's will. Even though we see people sick and dying we still believe God heals today. Even though we take medications, surgery and treatments we give God the glory since (supposedly) He guided the medical treatment. This is not biblical divine healing but a traditional Pentecostal teaching which is in error. It is not harmless to those who do not receive healing.

BRO. BAER: In some cases, I agree. The "healing movement" hijacked the initial Pentecostal movement, and most of the major Charismatic leaders who followed those early days became obsessed with healing... to the degree that many of them did not teach much doctrine, and present day proponents of extreme views of this don't seem to even have much conception of even the most basic biblical truths. The original seedbed of the Pentecostal movement was the Holiness movement, and much of it was later eclipsed by the healing movement and the associated health and wealth "gospel". If you are critiquing that, I am behind you my friend, but the fact that a great deal of hijacking of the message and power of Pentecost has occurred does not mean that the true power I, and many others, have personally seen and experienced is any less real. Yes, there are those who God may not have directly touched who regain their health, and there are even those who fake healings or are tricked into believing they have been or will be healed, but neither of those things eclipses the real spiritual exercise of God. Spiritual deception and pseudo-Pentecostal quackery does "muddy the water", but what is genuine is still genuine, in spite of the presence of fakery.

On your last, I deeply sympathize (and can empathize as well). I have seen wonderful children of God suffer without relief, and I have had several of the precious saints I have pastored die early deaths that were devastating to them, their families, and to our assembly. But, I have also seen supernatural interactions of God that **cannot** be denied due to the presence of the Spirit, multiple witnesses, **and** medical diagnoses given before and after from several independent doctors, labs, etc. Do I always understand, or can I always (even attempt to) explain why God appears to heal one person and not another? No, I cannot. But, lack of understanding on my part is not sufficient for me to reject the evidence and the simple fact that God does so (healing some while not healing others, even when the others seem more deserving in some cases) is more biblical than to believe He is not presently healing anyone. There are many biblical examples of God healing selectively and without a clear reason for that selection. That is how He worked all through the biblical period, so it is only consistent that we would see the same today.

BRO. M.M.: Hebrews 11 sheds some light on this subject.

Hebrews 11:35-40 *Women received their dead raised to life again: and others were tortured, not accepting deliverance; that they might obtain a better resurrection: And others had trial of cruel mockings and scourgings, yea, moreover of bonds and imprisonment: They were stoned, they were sawn asunder, were tempted, were slain with the sword: they wandered about in sheepskins and goatskins; being destitute, afflicted, tormented; (Of whom the world was not worthy:) they wandered in deserts, and in mountains, and in dens and caves of the earth. And these all, having obtained a good report through faith, received not the promise: God having provided some better thing for us, that they without us should not be made perfect.*

There is something great to be said about people of God that trust Him regardless of the outcome. You see Bro. M., it isn't all about everyone being healed every time to make it real. God picks and chooses what is best for us, even when we don't realize that it is in our own best interest. God is working on our spirits, and our bodies are only temporary vehicles to get us around in this life. We look for a better thing ahead. I'm sorry your wife didn't get healed, but it doesn't lessen God's ability to heal. When so many honest-hearted, Holy Ghost filled people are giving you personal experiences, it would pay to listen. I've been intently listening to these discussions, and while they are contrary to my belief on evil spirits, I respect these folks enough to at least consider what they say.

BRO. V.M.: Brethren, my message is simple: the gift of healing does not operate in the churches today, but a counterfeit does. It is a counterfeit that is erroneous and harmful to the Holy Ghost saints of God and should be exposed, which is my goal here. The peoples' characterization of their personal experiences and testimony is a result of allowing this counterfeit to operate all these years without correction, some believing that it is harmless. The ministry is to be blamed. Endless prayer lines without verifiable and demonstrable results is not healthy. While saints will claim their headache is healed, crippled, blind, wheelchair-bound and dying saints return dejected and confused. God cannot be pleased with this.

BRO. BAER: My message is simple as well my friend. I believe *both* exist in the church today: the genuine work of the Spirit (including healings) and counterfeit works as well. I completely agree that counterfeiting of the Spirit should be exposed and identified as such. I also believe that if we are not careful we can get our spiritual senses cauterized by a large number of emotion-driven experiences (emotionalism) rather than truly Spirit-driven experiences, which can affect our emotions, but which do not originate with our emotions but with the Spirit of God. I want the real thing, not a carnal imitation or emotional outburst cloaked as a move of the Spirit. We may have a powerfully emotional experience that is instigated by the Spirit, but we must be able to discern between the two (emotionalism only, versus the actual work of the Spirit that effects our emotions) as that has become a serious problem in Pentecostal (as we are) and Charismatic circles. I say that to parallel it with other operations of the Spirit. I believe that just like there are carnal expressions going on that are claimed to be spiritual *and* there are genuine spiritual expressions, so there are genuine healings of God, *and* natural recovery that God may or may not be directly involved in, *and* counterfeit (fake) "healings" and "miracles" that God is certainly not the author of. As to your continued claim that there are no genuine healings because you think that none of them are "verifiable and demonstrable", that claim is just as unsubstantiated by you as you claim it is by us. Many people (of which I am one) have seen demonstrable evidences of genuine healings. Many people have verifiable medical testimony (before and after prayer) that a condition is gone that was indisputably present, and in many cases has never returned. But, even if some pain, or other condition was taken away and then returned at some later point, the argument could still be made that God was providing relief (for a season) and not permanent healing in those cases.

The bottom line is that your claims that healings are not happening are just as subjective (and lacking of evidence) as you believe our claims are. The difference is that many of us *do* have medical evidence, multiple witnesses, and very clear experiential events that back up our claims, while you only have the argument that you personally (and subjectively) do not believe you personally have ever seen any true healings. Given the evidences we have, and how many of them there have been for so many of us, common sense should demand that you should not be dogmatically making the kinds of claims you are making (based on your personal experience alone) when the experiences of a great number of people completely contradict your own singular experience.

In addition, arguing that the evidences we have (direct experience, witnesses, and medical testimony) is insufficient to prove the validity of these healings is insensible. No outside neutral judge would consider those kinds of evidences insufficient. They are the only kinds of evidences that could be provided and are verifiable as real in exactly the same way (and with additional medical evidences as well) that the healing of the woman with the issue of blood being healed by Christ was. She experienced that healing, the Spirit's presence was noted, and witnesses attested to it. You don't deny Christ healed her, and she didn't even have some of the medical testimonies (tests, scans, etc.) that folks with the very same claims today have to back up those claims.

There is also no argument that can be made for your claims based on the fact that some (mysteriously) are not healed of dire conditions while others are healed. That was true all through the history of the Bible, so arguing that if that is true today that would have to mean that today's healings cannot be of God would require you to make the same claim about a number of healings in the Bible that are attributed to God by the biblical writers. My friend, please think about all of this. These simple facts obviate any argument you might have other than a prejudicial position based on personal subjective experience and feelings.

BRO. V.M.: Sometimes by not referencing certain comments it means I simply disagree, I am not ignoring them. Medical "evidence" of what, that God is so incomplete and lacking that He requires the advice and consent of doctors? I don't think so nor do I think a blind person requires a doctor to prove they can see, or the lame that they now walk or the crippled made straight.

BRO. BAER: Medical evidence is just a testimony (witness)… and it is you who have demanded those types of witnesses, so it is a bit odd that you are now writing them off as worthless. Of course it is not needed as any testimony to God. Of course we don't need a doctor to decide if what God did is real, but it is you, not us, that continues asking for verifiable evidence that a medical condition changed in a way that would seem to have to have been divinely instigated. In our assembly alone, I have several folks (before my time or during my time here) who have a very clear medical testimony that a very serious condition was present at the end of the week that (after being in a prayer service over the weekend) was not present at the beginning of the next week, and multiple medical doctors, tests, scans, etc. are evidence of that fact. Added to that was the response of the doctors themselves who were baffled at how a clearly present condition was gone, which is a powerful testimony in itself. We are not dependent on those medical testimonies to know a healing has occurred though, they are just "icing on the cake", additional witnesses to what we ourselves experienced. But, they are the kinds of empirical evidences you keep demanding and claiming we do not have... though we clearly do. The examples you are giving of major external issues are closer to the category of miracles than just simple healings, and I do not classify all healings in the same category. I do believe (though I know you don't believe this either) that the point will come when that level of the miraculous is occurring again as well.

BRO. V.M.: I do not believe that medical evidence has anything to do with divine healing. As I have said before, I know someone who is dying of cancer and has been given months to live. I despise having to even bring it up, but I know that their condition is so serious that I will repent of everything I have said regarding divine healing if this person survives. Many prayers and laying on of hands have taken place for the individual and this person has lived for God to their best all of their life. Even though I have requested anyone who believes they can heal this person to come, not one has agreed to do so.

BRO. A.M.: Can you hand out the Holy Ghost at will? If someone wanted it could you walk up at that second and give it to them? I'm beginning to think you don't understand how spiritual gifts work. Could any prophet, just at will, see whatever future he wanted? Could Peter walk on any water of his choosing? You act like God gave the apostles the power to hand out healing like candy. It never worked that way. Jesus raised three people from the dead during his entire ministry. Three. Are you saying that in three and a half years no one else died?

BRO. V.M.: If I had that gift, yes. I saw a man who claimed he had that gift was visiting our church. When he said that, he said he felt so much unbelief in the assembly that he requested permission from the minister to take a man who had been "tarrying" for many months into the back of the church. In just seconds, this man came running out into the church screaming, speaking in tongues and leaping into the air with joy! There was no doubt in my mind he had received it.

BRO. A.M.: I've known people who begged and pleaded, and cried and tarried for the Holy Ghost, sometimes for years. I don't know any that didn't get it, but the timetable isn't on us. God hands that out at His pleasure.

BRO. V.M.: Every single one who came for healing was healed. Shall I list them for you? Where did Jesus ever turn someone away asking him for healing?

BRO. A.M.: The beggar at the gate called beautiful, everyone that was waiting for Peter to walk by, almost all the people at the pool waiting for the angel to stir the waters, etc.

BRO. V.M.: The beggar was healed!

BRO. A.M.: Yes, but Jesus walked by him at least three times. Jesus left enough people unhealed that they were lining the streets for Peter.

BRO. BAER: Bro. V.M., I think (as Bro. A.M. appears to have pointed out) that you are confusing someone believing they have the gift of healing with God healing people. I make no claim to having the gift of healing, and I would question anyone presently making such a claim, but even if someone had that gift, that does not mean that they can heal people "at will" like some false prophets among the televangelists of our day seem to infer. You are blending their types of false claims with a simple belief that God still does heal, though for His own reasons (that are not always easy to understand) and through whatever vessel (or none at all) that He chooses to use to be involved in the process. No one here is claiming that we have the ability to heal whomever we want, or even that any one of us is specially used in that way on a consistent basis. We are simply pointing out that God does still presently heal (at His own discretion) and sometimes that is done through the laying on of hands, etc.

We (a large group of ministers and saints) had several intense prayer services for some very dire cases (almost certainly including the one I believe you are referring to) in the meeting I just got home from a week ago. Were they healed? I do not know. I am not the arbiter of whether someone gets healed. God is. I pray that they were or will be. Many cases of this kind we have faced have not been healed, but some *have* definitively and unquestionably been healed. Will I erase the validity of healings that did occur because others did not? No, I will not. Will I question whether God still heals (when I have seen Him do so) because there are times He does not heal, and I (a finite human) do not understand why He doesn't? No, I will not.

Jesus did not heal everyone who needed healing. The very fact that those of his home region would not accept him limited many of them from the possibility of being healed. It was due in their case to a lack of faith... which is what troubles me about your claims, and is one of many reasons you may not believe you have experienced healing (and may not have).

Mark 6:5 *And he could there do no mighty work, save that he laid his hands upon* ***a few*** *sick folk, and healed them.*

He even pointed out this very thing in Luke's account.

Luke 4:25-27 *But I tell you of a truth, many widows were in Israel in the days of Elias, when the heaven was shut up three years and six months, when great famine was throughout all the land; But* ***unto none of them was Elias sent, save unto Sarepta****, a city of Sidon, unto a woman that was a widow. And many lepers were in Israel in the time of Eliseus the prophet; and* ***none of them was cleansed, saving Naaman the Syrian****.*

BRO. V.M.: Must I list them again!?

Matthew 4:24 *And his fame went throughout all Syria: and they brought unto him all sick people that were taken with divers diseases and torments, and those which were possessed with devils, and those which were lunatick, and those that had the palsy; and he healed them.*

Not one scripture proves anyone was ever denied healing.

BRO. BAER: It is unfortunate that you apply hyperbole to the language of passages you don't agree with (as you have in discussing other subjects as well), but don't seem to see (or just don't want to see) it in passages where it would qualify your conclusions. The fact that Jesus is described as healing all who were brought unto him at one time or in one location does not mean that was true in all cases, at all times, and in all locations. It was true either literally or hyperbolically in the location where he was at in **Matthew 4:24**, but that has no bearing on how things were at other times or in other locations. And, if you want to take this hyper-literally, you do realize he only (according to the hyper-literal use of this language) healed those who were "brought unto him". What about all those folks who were in such terrible shape (perhaps lying on their deathbeds at home) that they couldn't be "brought unto him"? Were *they* all healed? You are not thinking through the conclusions of your statements. Clearly there were folks who needed to be healed who were not healed simply because Jesus was healing many.

And Bro. A.M. is absolutely right. Jesus apparently did not heal the many other sick folks gathered around the pool of Bethesda, choosing to heal only one of them.

BRO. A.M.: That means that Jesus looked at the other others and didn't see fit to heal them.

BRO. V.M.: No one who approached Jesus or anyone else were denied healing, not one!

Matthew 8:16 *When the even was come, they brought unto him many that were possessed with devils: and he cast out the spirits with his word, and healed all that were sick:*

Luke 6:19 *And the whole multitude sought to touch him: for there went virtue out of him, and healed them all.*

BRO. BAER: Now your argument is that the only way they can receive healing is to approach him? Once again, what about the many folks who may have been physically incapacitated and could not approach him? I'm sure the very worst cases were in that exact kind of situation: bedridden at home and without the kinds of folks who could lower them through the roof to bring them to Jesus as in the case of the lame man. There is no doubt that the most dire cases could not approach him themselves, and many may not have even had anyone who could appeal to him on their behalf. So only the mobile and non-bedridden deserve healing? Only those with enough friends to bring them to him (so they can "approach" him)? Your prejudices against the possibility of healing demand a great number of serious logical fallacies and biblical inconsistencies.

Added to that is a serious misunderstanding of the word "all", not only in that all in one place does not mean all in all places, but also that the word "all" in the Bible does not always mean every single one everywhere. Misusing the word "all" in an overly literal way can be highly misleading. As just one example, the Scripture says that *all* Judaea were *all* baptized by John.

Mark 1:5 *And there went out unto him **all** the land of Judaea, and they of Jerusalem, and were **all** baptized of him in the river of Jordan, confessing their sins.*

There are several examples of the hyperbolic way "all" can be used in the Gospels that are demonstrated in this statement. Do you really believe that *all* the inhabitants in the land of Judah and *all* the folks in Jerusalem came to hear John? Do you really believe that that *all* those who came to hear John were even *all* baptized by him?

It is certain that the "all" in both of these statements is a hyperbolic way of saying "all" that is not intended to mean every single individual person. Some folks in Judaea and Jerusalem may not have even been physically capable of going to see John (due to age or infirmity). Undoubtedly there were those who came to hear him that were not baptized, which is proved by his references to those who came with the wrong motives not bringing forth fruit meet for repentance (**Matthew 3:7-8**).

The word "all" in these kinds of contexts simply refers to folks from "all over" or even the ***overall*** group. Regardless of whether this is meant in the same way in some of the statements regarding Jesus' work (and there is no viable reason to claim it cannot be, based on the use of the very same word "all" above), it does demonstrate that "all" does not always mean "every single one".

BRO. V.M.: Acts 5:16 *There came also a multitude out of the cities round about unto Jerusalem, bringing sick folks, and them which were vexed with unclean spirits: and they were healed every one.*

BRO. BAER: Even if it could be argued that there were times that "every (single) one" was healed who was sick, that does not prove that every one or all were healed that were sick in every place and circumstance. Bro. A.M. has several times mentioned the pool of Bethesda as an example, and there are other similar examples. But, once again, what about all the folks that were so sick or shut in that they couldn't come to Jesus or had no one who could bring them to him? If that is your whole argument: that Jesus always healed everyone everywhere in every circumstance, that claim is very easily disproved by a simple study of the Bible. What bearing does that have on his disciples' later healings you referred to? There were obviously many saints who died during the period of Peter and Paul's ministry, and even folks they themselves didn't appear able to heal (that they were requesting prayer for), so there is no basis for the argument you are trying to make: that if healing is present today, everyone who needs healing and comes to Jesus will automatically be healed. Let alone is it viable to argue that everyone who is a man of God would have that ability in our day. Where is discernment in this widescale expectation of healing you believe in? What if someone was sick because of God's judgement and God intended them to be sick for the next year? Would all they have to do is "approach Jesus and they would be healed, even if God Himself had intended them to be sick? You did say that everyone (with no exception) who "approached" Jesus for healing was healed after all. Would those under judgment or simply those God was taking through a process by allowing them to be sick be healed if they came to Jesus in the crowd seeking healing? Of course not. It is blinding prejudice towards your unbiblical presuppositions that is causing you to make these kinds of arguments. Simple biblical evidence and rational consideration should cause you to cease making them.

BRO. A.M.: I will say this discussion has opened my mind up to see more scriptures where Jesus didn't heal everyone. The woman with the issue of blood was the only person in that crowd recorded healed. There was a man at a synagogue that Jesus healed in front of the Pharisees on the Sabbath. No one else was recorded healed. This whole conversation is reminding me of the end of the book of Job. Job wanted a chance with God to ask why. When God showed up, He declares His majesty, His works, and His wisdom, but never explained why Job suffered.

BRO. BAER: Bro. V.M., let me summarize a few of the claims you have been making and the problems they have.

You have claimed that since you personally do not believe you have ever seen a healing by God in our day, they must not exist. The fact that you personally do not believe you have ever seen a divine healing is not sufficient evidence to override the fact that many of us claim that we have. It is merely your subjective and personal experience, which is, especially in the light of many contradictory witnesses, no evidence at all.

You have claimed that divine healing does not presently occur because it is unreasonable to conclude that God would heal some folks (some of which may have minor issues) while not healing other folks (some of which may have major issues). The certainty that God *does* heal some while not healing others is a simple biblical fact. Sometimes He heals only one person, who may or may not be "worthy" of that healing, or who may not have as serious a condition as others who might be more "worthy" or even more (in our understanding) in need. We find this precedent in both the Old and New Testament periods, so there is no basis for arguing that present day healings are not real because God would not heal someone of minor issues while not healing someone else of a major issue. He did that very thing all through the Bible.

You have claimed that divine healing does not presently occur because there are examples of "supposed" divine healings which are clearly counterfeit. The fact that there are counterfeited claims of the Spirit's activity have no bearing whatsoever on whether or not the Spirit is presently active. In fact, it is more likely to assume that these counterfeits are intended to distract from and diminish the reality of the genuine work of the Spirit. Added to that is the fact that there have always been, all through history, counterfeit claims of healing and supernatural activity. During the very time that God and Christ were healing individuals, there were pagan religious priests and adherents claiming supernatural activity as well (including supposed healings). Thus, the presence of the counterfeit in our day is not evidence that there is no real work of the Spirit of this kind as that same evidence was present in the days of the Bible when God was working through His Spirit.

You appear to claim that the Bible supports your belief in the permanent (or at least present) cessation of Spirit directed healing. The fact that you yourself still believe in the baptism of the Holy Spirit in the same way it operated in the early church period undermines your entire claim that healing has ceased, as it is clear that the level of the work of the Holy Spirit present in the first century A.D. also "ceased", or at the very least was much less available, for a long period of time, and was restored (at least in a larger corporate sense) at the end of the 19th century A.D. and the beginning of the 20th century A.D. That alone demonstrates the inconsistent nature of your claims.

Not only is your interpretation inconsistent with your own experience, you are *basing it* on your own experience, which is even more dangerous. You claimed that you know tongues and Holy Spirit baptism is present because *you* personally experienced it, but that healing is not present because *you* have not personally experienced it. Your personal experiences alone are not the litmus test for the presence of God's Spirit and spiritual operations, and they certainly aren't sufficient to ignore the personal experiences of many thousands, if not millions, of other individuals. If your personal experience of the baptism of the Holy Spirit is good enough for you to believe it is present, then you have no right to argue against the personal experiences of others in regard to healing. The fact that you have not personally experienced it does not make it any less real than the fact that there are many Christians who have not personally experienced the baptism of the Holy Spirit, and who make the same claims about it that you are making about healings.

The preceding very simply proves that the majority of your claims for why divine healings are not occurring presently are invalid, or at the very least insufficient to make such claims. If you have any better reasons for your very dogmatic (and to some, offensive to God) claims, particularly if they are biblically based, then I hope you will give them and we can discuss them.

BRO. V.M.: In every case where multitudes came to be healed they were all healed. Period. Exclamation point. Now you can return to your cocoon of unscriptural belief.

BRO. A.M.: At the pool of Bethesda one man was healed (out of a multitude of sick people). Out of the crowd thronging Jesus, only the woman with the issue of blood was healed. Period. Exclamation point. End of story.

BRO. M.M.: Matthew 13:57-58 *And they were offended in him. But Jesus said unto them, A prophet is not without honour, save in his own country, and in his own house. And he did not many mighty works there because of their unbelief.*

BRO. V.M.: Again, show me one single person ever turned away who sought healing. I can make the answer easy if you like, not one single person, period. Yet multitudes were healed, every one!

BRO. A.M.: You are just ignoring the cases we have shared with you where Jesus didn't heal every single one because it doesn't fit into your world view.

BRO. V.M.: No, you are ignoring the multitudes who were healed, every one! No one was ever turned away! No healing ever failed! There is nothing even close to that today and you can't face up to it. I truly feel sorry for you, your programming is complete.

No one who sought healing was ever turned away! No healing ever failed!

I know someone who is dying as I have already explained, and you are aware of it. This person is young with young children, loves God, has the Holy Ghost, served

God all of their life. Tell me, what effort are you making to facilitate the healing of this person? Why don't you bring your healing belief here to my church and facilitate their healing? Why haven't you even offered to? When are you coming?

Is Jesus choosing to leave this person unhealed, is that your answer?

BRO. BAER: Bro. V.M., it does appear (as you seem to be accusing those who believe in healings) that discussing this with you is an uphill battle that cannot be won. Not because you are right, but because you are unable to do more than repeat claims which have been refuted, and refuse to address claims which contradict your beliefs. I am sorry that is the case, not because I want to disprove your position on this, but because your conception of the biblical and historical record is so skewed and bent towards your belief that it is heartbreaking. I just gave you a list of reasons why your claims are not proof of your conclusion. They are simple facts that contradict the way you continue looking at this issue, and they cannot be overridden by your biased personal feelings or subjective personal experiences. It appears that you have now defaulted to two continuous claims, neither of which prove your conclusion. First, your belief that Jesus healed every single person who ever came to him for healing. And second, that if God is still healing today, the only proof of it is that we should go heal every person who is suffering and worthy of healing. On the first of these, you have no idea if that is true as all you can do (and have done) is quote passages that appear to state that in certain places, at certain times in his ministry "all" or "everyone" who came to him was healed. That does not prove that every single time throughout his entire ministry every single person who came to him was healed. Nor does it prove that every single time anyone later came to the apostles (who you agree were healing some people) they were healed (the Bible very clearly contradicts that). You have no evidence whatsoever to make that case, as all we know is that "all" (however we define that word, and I showed you it can mean something other than "every single one" in the Bible) at *that time* and in *that place* were healed.

Added to that (which by itself obviates your "all people at all places at all times who came to him were always healed" argument) is the fact that we have given you a number of biblical examples where he clearly left folks unhealed who needed healing: in his home country, at the pool of Bethesda, any and all who simply were not physically capable of coming to him or did not have anyone who could bring them to him, etc. These last would be especially heartbreaking as they are likely the ones who needed him most (who are in such desperate physical condition that they not only cannot make it to him, but that they have no one to bring them to him either).

How do you account for these folks, who needed him in a greater way even than those who made their way to him, but who apparently went unhealed?

As to your second claim, it is wrongly based on the skewed way you are paralleling the healings Jesus carried out in his day to the healings of this day. Jesus in person and in the purpose he was carrying out in the short period of his earthly ministry would clearly have been doing things at a scale that we would not be doing in our day, especially if (as you reject due to more examples of skewed interpretation) the church has not been restored yet (to the level of what the early church was). Why in the world should we expect that the level and scale of healings in our day would equal that of Jesus in the small window of his earthly ministry? I would imagine most of us would never make such a case nor would any of us argue that we have some "instant on" or "always on" ability to heal (as that appears to be how your incorrectly define a healing gift). Thus, your argument that we aren't doing things at the level Jesus was is meaningless. Of course we're not (at least not *yet*). And, your argument that if we believe in the possibility of healings we should come and pray for this precious sister, you are seriously misrepresenting our position. To begin with, if who you are referring to is who I believe you are, we did have a very intensive prayer (that included many ministers) with her in person less than two weeks ago. None of us are claiming that because we believe God still does heal that we are able to make Him heal though, or that our prayers are so personally powerful that whoever we pray for will be healed. Why do you continue making such false misrepresentations of our belief? Why would it be necessary for us to believe such a thing simply because we believe God presently still heals?

I have seen many not healed, but I *have* seen people healed. We (those of us you continue to challenge to heal people) are *not* the source of healing, and none of us are claiming the personal power to heal anyone, but we know that God can do so through whomever He chooses or through no one at all. So enough of these challenges when they are simply misdirection and misrepresentation of what we actually believe. We do not believe we can heal at will, though God can. We do not believe that our personal prayers are a guarantee of results, but if God chooses to act (and He has done so in our day) then there will be results.

So, the handful of passages you keep quoting about Jesus healing "all" does not prove what you are claiming. It might be hyperbolic but, regardless of that, it definitely is not a description used every single time he was healing, and there are a number of cases where he clearly left many unhealed.

That is not the only contradiction to your assumptions in the biblical record though. During the height of the work of the early church, when Paul and Peter were still both alive and actively working, both of them only raised *one single* recorded person from the dead (in their entire ministry as far as the Bible records). I am certain there were many precious saints who died during their day (of age, illness, accidents, persecution, etc.) from the very beginning of the period of the work of the early church to its end. Clearly, they were not healing "all" and "every (single) one". There were also several cases where Paul mentioned conditions that some of his own disciples and co-laborers were suffering with that they clearly had not been healed of (**1 Timothy 5:23**). One of these examples (where he left someone behind sick) occurred in the same time period when great miracles were occurring and dead were raised (**2 Timothy 2:40**). That is the simplest evidence in the world that God's healing is an "all" or nothing thing. That either "all" get healed who need healed, or God is not healing at all. Not "all" who needed healing were healed in the days of Christ or in the days of the early church. Both the full testimony of Jesus' activity and the testimony of that of the leaders of the early church proves that they were not healing every single person that needed healing. So, even if (which we are not claiming) we had the same scale of power they had, why in the world would you expect anyone in our day to be doing something that they themselves were not even doing (healing every single case in every single place at every single time)? Your biased view leaves you blinded to those simple biblical facts that entirely contradict your claims.

But, there is another far more important and very simple thing that you appear blind to. The Lord has never healed every single person at every single time in every single place who needed and desired to be healed, including those who "came to him" (which seems to be your prerequisite requirement for them being healed). As I already pointed out, that would have no meaning to someone who could not "come" or "be brought" to Jesus.

There is a simple reason why this is true, and that (along with all the other evidences) you seem to have blinded yourself to. No matter how much someone needs or wants healing, the Lord alone is the source of divine healing and the Lord alone is the one making the decision whether or not someone will be healed (based on factors we most often could not even begin to comprehend). Healing has never been the "norm" in a cursed world. It is an exception to the rule of life under the curse, not the rule and normative expectation.

The Lord may not heal someone for a number of reasons that preclude every single person at all times who "comes to him" being healed. For one, what if someone who

God intended to remain in an unhealed state "came to Jesus" for healing? Wouldn't Jesus be contradicting God's will if that person was under judgement, going through a process that God intended, etc., and they were among the "all" that Jesus healed? God may have a reason why a person is in the condition they are in. It could be due to judgement. It could be due to His desire to take them through a process that, until it is complete, no amount of "coming to the Lord" and requesting healing will override it. It could be for the purpose of others to witness their healing, and until the time that those others who He wants to witness it are present, them coming to the Lord to request healing will not cause Him to act. It could be for many other far more mysterious (to us) reasons as well. Some he takes away (through death) so that they will not have to go through something in their day, or what is coming in the future. I have known several who could not have taken some of the things that occurred not long after they passed who escaped those things by death.

Regardless of His reasons, He does not always heal everyone, as there may be a purpose for their going through their condition that we simply do not understand, and for many other reasons as well.

So, the bottom line is that none of the arguments you are (unfortunately and illogically) making change the biblical precedents and examples we have given. You can cherry-pick a few passages that appear to say that Jesus healed "all" or "every (single) one", but those passages do not change the message of the many examples of the exact opposite being the case with Jesus and the leaders of the early church. You are simply choosing statements that you think (wrongly) support your belief while entirely ignoring the many others that very definitely do not. And, as I have pointed out several times, these are only less than a handful of examples of less than a handful of occurrences in the three and a half year period of Jesus' ministry where this language of "all" and "every" is even used, which, once again, proves nothing about whether or not this was always the case in all places. And, in the at least forty-year period of the early church, when its principal leaders were still living, we find the same things that entirely contradict your claims: powerful healings and even the dead being raised, but at the same time some who were not being healed who were clearly in need of healing and were good and godly people.

ARI'EL INSTITUTE

SPEAKING IN TONGUES:
TONGUES and an "UNKNOWN" TONGUE

BRO. A.M: Why do we rarely hear any teaching about praying for understanding when it comes to speaking in tongues? Paul mentioned this in **1 Corinthians 14**, but I've never really heard anyone talk about it in length.

BRO. BAER: Can you expand on this Bro. M.?

BRO. A.M.: Paul adjures us to pray in tongues but to also pray for understanding. I often see people praying in tongues but never hear anyone talking about what that specific exchange meant. That verse seems to imply that when I pray in tongues I ought to understand what the Spirit was praying about. I often forget to do this myself and I can't think of a time that I've heard anyone either preach or testify as to something they heard or felt when praying in tongues.

1 Corinthians 14:13-17 *Wherefore let him that speaketh in an unknown tongue pray that he may interpret. For if I pray in an unknown tongue, my spirit prayeth, but my understanding is unfruitful. What is it then? I will pray with the spirit, and I will pray with the understanding also: I will sing with the spirit, and I will sing with the understanding also. Else when thou shalt bless with the spirit, how shall he that occupieth the room of the unlearned say Amen at thy giving of thanks, seeing he understandeth not what thou sayest? For thou verily givest thanks well, but the other is not edified.*

BRO. V.M.: 1 Corinthians 14:27-28 *If any man speak in an unknown tongue, let it be by two, or at the most by three, and that by course; and let one interpret. But if there be no interpreter, let him keep silence in the church; and let him speak to himself, and to God.*

BRO. A.M.: This is the part that I'm specifically focusing on: "For if I pray in an unknown tongue, my spirit prayeth, but my understanding is unfruitful. What is it then? I will pray with the spirit, and I will pray with the understanding also". The implication seems to be that if we pray or speak in tongues we ought to be praying for understanding. Otherwise, we are just making noise.

BRO. V.M.: I believe Paul is addressing an unhealthy emphasis on tongues by balancing both ways of prayer, but not degrading either. There seemed to be an overzealous use of tongues in the church as he addresses this in other places as well.

BRO. BAER: I agree.

BRO. E.F.: Well I was raised Pentecost, but a lot of Pentecost lacks understanding of the difference between unknown tongues and other tongues. The unknown tongue is just that, and is no dialect in this world but is a holy language. The only way you can understand it is if God uses someone to interpret it.

BRO. V.M.: There are no tongues that are a known human language.

1 Corinthians 14:2 *For he that speaketh in an unknown tongue speaketh not unto men, but unto God: for no man understandeth him; howbeit in the spirit he speaketh mysteries.*

BRO. E.F.: Bro. M., you need to know there were other tongues spoken on Pentecost and unknown tongues that Paul spoke **1 Corinthians 14:2**. They were speaking in other tongues on the day of Pentecost, and the devout Jews understood what they were saying, and knew that it had to be God because they were Galileans who spoke Aramaic.

BRO. V.M.: You are mistaken. There is only one tongue and no one but God or a saint with the gift of interpretation can understand it.

BRO. BAER: Bro. F. is not mistaken. There are "tongues" (plural).

Mark 16:17 *And these signs shall follow them that believe; In my name shall they cast out devils; they shall speak with new **tongues**;*

Acts 2:4 *And they were all filled with the Holy Ghost, and began to speak with other **tongues**, as the Spirit gave them utterance.*

Acts 2:11 *Cretes and Arabians, we do hear them speak in our **tongues** the wonderful works of God.*

Acts 10:46 *For they heard them speak with **tongues**, and magnify God....*

Acts 19:6 *And when Paul had laid his hands upon them, the Holy Ghost came on them; and they spake with **tongues**, and prophesied.*

1 Corinthians 12:30 Have all the gifts of healing? do all speak with **TONGUES**? do all interpret?

1 Corinthians 13:1 *Though I speak with the **tongues** of men and of angels, and have not charity, I am become as sounding brass, or a tinkling cymbal.*

1 Corinthians 13:8 *Charity never faileth: but whether there be prophecies, they shall fail; whether there be **tongues**, they shall cease; whether there be knowledge, it shall vanish away.*

1 Corinthians 14:5-6 *I would that ye all spake with **tongues**, but rather that ye prophesied: for greater is he that prophesieth than he that speaketh with **tongues**, except he interpret, that the church may receive edifying. Now, brethren, if I come unto you speaking with **tongues**, what shall I profit you, except I shall speak to you either by revelation, or by knowledge, or by prophesying, or by doctrine?*

1 Corinthians 14:18 *I thank my God, I speak with **tongues** more than ye all:*

On these last two examples in **1 Corinthians 14**, Paul refers to himself as individually speaking in tongues (plural): one person speaking in multiple tongues. In the same chapter, he also refers to speaking in a single tongue (**1 Corinthians 14:14**), which proves that he could speak in one tongue or more than one tongue (tongues) when in the Spirit. Other examples in that same chapter are in **1 Corinthians 14:21-23, 14:39**, etc. The use of the plural "tongues" clearly refers to a multiplicity of different languages. That is simply how it is used in the Bible. Just consider the exact same type of plural from and grammar used with that terminology in **Genesis 10:20, 10:31, Isaiah 66:18, Revelation 7:9, 10:11, 11:9, 13:7, 17:15,** etc.

BRO. S.O. (Uganda): As clear as that! However, you must take note that, Spirit baptism comes in two ways; in the tongues of men, and of angels (**1 Corinthians 13:1**). In that none of us is an angel, we cannot interpret an angelic tongue speaking child of God.

BRO. BAER: Though many have made the distinction that Bro. F. referenced between "other tongues" and an "unknown tongue", I have not often heard Bro. M.'s belief (if I understood it correctly, which I may not have) that no tongues are human tongues (languages), and that there is only one tongue. Brethren, please correct my misunderstanding if I am stating this incorrectly. The first of these beliefs (what Bro. F. referred to) is very common among us, but I do not see it quite as it has been commonly taught. It is based on language the *King James Version* translators added to the Bible that was not in the original text. The only time that the phrase "unknown tongue" is used in the *King James Version* is in **1 Corinthians 14** (in **1 Corinthians**

14:2, 14:4, 14:13-14, 14:19, and 14:27). In every example it is in italics in the *King James Version*. When the *King James Version* translators added their own words that were not in the original Greek (or Hebrew, etc.) manuscripts of the Bible, they put those words in italics so it would be clear that they were adding either what amounted to "filler" to make the sentences more readable in English or to clarify what *they* believed was meant by a statement. This is ***not*** what the Bible actually said, but what amounts to their own commentary in the text to fill in blanks they believed needed to be filled in. Thus, there is actually no "unknown tongue" referred to anywhere in the Bible. The references in **1 Corinthians 14** that are noted above should all simply read "tongue" as the word "unknown" is not in the original; the only word in the original text of **1 Corinthians 14** is "tongue". So, we actually have no biblical reason to believe in an "unknown" tongue, though there are certainly "tongues" (languages) that are human or possibly even angelic that are "unknown" to us, simply meaning we don't speak or understand them, and in some cases may never have heard them.

I do personally believe in both the tongues of men (human languages) and the tongue of angels (the "native" language of celestial beings), based in part on a statement in the preceding chapter.

1 Corinthians 13:1 *Though I speak with **the tongues of men and of angels**....*

It would make little sense for this to be a reference to someone who is able to speak English and Spanish (being multi-lingual), etc. This clearly refers to speaking in tongues under the inspiration of the Holy Spirit and seems to imply that not only could someone potentially speak in other human languages but they could speak in the language of the celestial realm (that which angels apparently speak in their native communication).

Though I fully agree that the idea behind speaking in tongues in prayer or praise to God (as communication with God) would seem most normally to be in a language that would ***not*** be understood by others (as the conversation is just between you and God), I do not think that would require that it only be in a language that has never been heard by humans. If someone was speaking in Japanese and there was not a single person present who spoke Japanese, then it might as well be an "unknown" tongue in that environment, as no one present knows it (making it "unknown" to them).

There have been many examples in the history of the Pentecostal movement in which someone speaking in tongues was doing so in a language which could be understood by other humans, and apparently God allowed that for the purpose as a witness to those hearing it. This was the case on the day of Pentecost.

Acts 2:6-8 *...every man heard them speak **in his own language**. And they were all amazed and marvelled, saying one to another, Behold, are not all these which speak Galilaeans? And how hear we every man **in our own tongue**, wherein we were born?*

This has been the case at other times throughout history as well, as there have been many testimonies of folks who were present when someone else was worshiping God in tongues (not just speaking directly to other humans, but speaking to God) and they heard them praising God in their language, which they recognized, and which they knew the speaker did not know how to speak. This has also happened in a more direct way when someone spoke in a human language they did not know to a person who did know it in order to demonstrate to that person that it was the Spirit inspiring that communication. The father of Bro. Moore (the pastor of the Gospel Assembly Church in Green, Ohio) had this exact experience.

BRO. V.M.: Just for the record, this is simply another ancient Pentecostal fable. The miracle (in **Acts 2**) was in the hearing: that every man heard the same speakers simultaneously in the language they were born in.

BRO. BAER: I'm sorry my friend, but that is not at all consistent with the actual words of **Acts 2**. The fact that they spoke in languages and dialects that could be understood by these varied dispersia Jews is simply what the passage states. I can't "hear" someone speak in English unless they actually speak in English. If I hear them speak in Spanish it is because they are speaking Spanish. There is no basis for arguing that they were not speaking English or Spanish, but that I just heard those languages. What would be the point of that? It is much simpler for God to just let a person speak in the actual language that He wants the other person to hear them speak. But, I realize you have to see it that way if you are laboring under the misconception that there is only one single "other tongue" and not truly "other tongues" being spoken. I believe you are heavily over-complicating the simple meaning of the passage. It seems that (whether on this subject or many others) you simply are never satisfied with any traditional or commonly held understanding and are always seeking a different or "better" (in your opinion) view than anyone else has ever had. I completely agree that there are things which time and tradition has blurred and has blinded much of Christendom to, but that does not mean that everything has to have some counter-contextual and mysterious meaning. Some things just are what they are, and most believe them the way they do because they are not complicated or mysterious: they just mean what they simply say.

I mean no insult at all by that as I greatly respect the desire to seek deeper truth, and fully agree with the necessity to question all traditions, going completely "back to the Bible". That is paramount, especially if we are seeking to have the truth and order of that first church (the early church). But, many things that have been believed a certain way are believed that way because that is simply what the Bible says. We do not need to reinvent or reject every commonly understood interpretation *if* those commonly understood interpretations are biblically faithful and the most obvious and sensible meaning of the Scripture.

BRO. V.M.: I keep many subjects, as Bro. J.S. taught, "on a shelf", not having the answer to await a better time and additional knowledge.

BRO. BAER: I do as well my friend.

BRO. R.A.: I have some big questions in the area of tongues. I wholeheartedly agree with the baptism of the Holy Ghost with the evidence of speaking in tongues. My biggest question from my observations in many services is that at times what is regarded as "speaking in tongues" seems to be along the lines of glossolalia or a "learned" language. I do not believe this is "as the Spirit gives utterance". I may be in error about this, but just giving my honest feelings on the matter. I do often wonder about this and need help on this question.

BRO. V.M.: The only time I have ever heard what I absolutely know was authentic speaking in tongues is when I was alone in my apartment and receiving the gift of the Holy Ghost. Since then I have heard imitation tongues which are people who have learned to utter words to imitate authentic tongues because they have been taught that they are supposed to continue speaking in tongues and they have peer pressure from fellow church goers demonstrating fake tongues. These errant people believe they are authentic, they are deceived.

BRO. BAER: First of all, the very fact that you claim that the only time you have heard authentic speaking in tongues is when you yourself were doing it, and no one else you have ever heard speaking in tongues (apparently other than yourself) was truly doing so... is a very troubling claim, and you may want to reconsider (or consider for the first time if you never have) what that kind of statement infers and how it may sound to others.

Yes, there are times when what is thought to be worship in the Spirit is only emotionalism or even repetitive mimicry of speaking in tongues, but that does not obviate the presence of the actual. There have always been emotion-driven experiences that (most of the time unknown to those having them) were an imitation of the actual, and not the actual. But, emotions will always be involved in our worship and are part of the human expression of a true encounter with the actual Spirit. There is certainly a difference between emotionalism and emotion which is generated by the Spirit. By the first, I simply mean that sometimes folk's emotionalism is what produces the feelings they are associating with the Spirit. If it is the true Spirit though, your emotions will certainly be involved. That is part of why God created the human emotional package: to interact with man and to allow man to feel what He feels. That said, I think it is a dangerous thing to claim that an encounter someone has, that they and others around them are certain is the Spirit, is not the Spirit. If it is the Spirit, denying its reality and operation comes perilously close to spiritual blasphemy.

BRO. R.A.: I also wonder about the amount of emphasis the Scripture places on speaking in tongues. Over and over again in Acts it is mentioned alongside being filled with the Holy Ghost and/or prophesying, and Paul discusses it in Corinthians. Outside of that, the topic is largely not addressed. If we did not have the Corinthian scriptures, we would be severely lacking for scriptures on the topic, outside of the book of Acts. If it is of utmost importance that we speak in tongues *after* Holy Ghost baptism, why is nearly every other New Testament book silent on the topic? I think that speaking in tongues has often been so emphasized that people resort to a "learned" language versus "as the Spirit gives utterance". Again, just honest thoughts, I hope to stimulate some discussion on this.

BRO. V.M.: I agree and would say the exact same thing with other "learned traditions" such as divine healing. Also, in almost fifty years among Holy Ghost filled people I have never once heard what I believed to be authentic tongues or interpretation. Neither have I witnessed what I believed to be a divine healing.

BRO. BAER: Bro. M., your last statements are the product of your rejection of elements of the supernatural realm, many of which millions of people have experienced. You have supported that unsustainable idea with a massive and heavy handed allegorical and (forgive me) many times insensible (in terms of rationality and language) rewriting of the simple and straightforward statements of the Scripture with allegorical and figurative meanings… which, even if they could be made, do not obviate the obvious primary meanings of those passages. It is that methodology that has produced your highly questionable (and potentially heretical) conceptions of the work of the Spirit (whether related to speaking in tongues, healing, etc.).

You can only come to the conclusions that you do by rewriting or overwriting the clear and primary meaning of scriptural statements. Given that we have discussed these subjects in great detail and have provided many biblical statements that contradict your conclusions, and you have never given an inch on any interpretation of your own, it appears that no amount of evidence disproving those acts of revision and rejection is enough evidence for you to consider your ways. We have given many evidences that completely contradict your claims on these subjects. Many times these claims you are making are entirely opinion driven and entirely without biblical support, unless of course, you change or ignore the meaning of biblical statements and create your own personal rules of biblical language and grammar.

As to Bro. A.'s points above, they are very important to consider. Tongues are not the object of our spiritual operation, they are a part of that operation. As they relate to the audible evidence of Holy Spirit baptism, they *cannot* be overemphasized. As they relate to the corporate activity of the church, it is certainly true that they *can* be overemphasized. That is exactly what Paul is addressing in **1 Corinthians 14**. Not that there is only "one (unknown) tongue" and no human "tongues" spoken in the church (which is disproved by the very words of that chapter), and not that tongues are not a normative part of worship. What he is saying is that "all things" (including speaking in tongues) should be done decently and in order. Speaking in tongues (plural) is part of the ***all things*** in **1 Corinthians 14:40** that *are done* as part of the operation of the church; the only point being added that they be only done decently and in order: in the right way (real and not put on or "learned") and at the right time (when the Spirit is present for that purpose).

Bro. M., some of these claims you are making (such as your claim that there is only one single "tongue" people speak in when speaking in tongues, and it is never a human tongue or plural tongues) are the very reason why I keep bringing the point back up that we have to use proper language and grammar. If the following is not correct, then please prove that biblically. But, if the following is correct, then it would be best to concede that a person can speak with more than one tongue.

The term "tongue" (in the singular) is principally used in **1 Corinthians 14**. Otherwise the term "tongues" is generally used for "speaking in tongues". The singular "tongue" referred to in **1 Corinthians 14** does not prove that there is only one single "tongue" that people speak in when speaking in tongues as the rest of the chapter refers to "tongues" (plural) being spoken. All of the following statements (and those addressing a "tongue" as well) are much easier to comprehend if you simply replace the word "tongue" with "language", which is what it is referring to: thus, speaking in another "language", or speaking in other "languages". Either could be true. A person can be speaking in another "language" (other than their own) or in other "languages" (other than their own).

1 Corinthians 14:5 says, "I would that ye all spoke with *tongues*". It does not say, "I would that you all spoke in the tongue (or even a tongue)". In the very same verse it says "he (singular) which speaketh with tongues (plural)". That alone proves that one person can speak in more than one tongue.

The very next verse says, "if I (singular) come unto you speaking with tongues (plural)". That also, all by itself, proves that one person can speak in more than one tongue when speaking in tongues.

In **1 Corinthians 14:18** Paul says, "I thank my God, I (singular) speak with tongues (plural) more than ye all". The very next verse demonstrates how Paul is using this term in both the singular and plural when he says, "Yet in the church I had rather speak five words with my understanding… than ten thousand words in an unknown tongue." In other words, Paul stated that he spoke in "tongues" (plural) in **1 Corinthians 14:18** and then referred to speaking in one of those plural tongues when he said "a tongue" (again, there is no "unknown tongue" in the Bible, just "a tongue") in the very next verse. Paul spoke in other languages in worship, but speaking in a language that could be understood by its hearers in teaching was more productive for the corporate church than him speaking in a language unknown by others would be.

1 Corinthians 14:21 clarifies this even further and clearly contradicts your claim regarding human languages not being spoken when speaking in tongues.

1 Corinthians 14:21-22 *In the law it is written, With men of other **tongues** (plural) and other lips will I speak unto this people… Wherefore **tongues** (plural) are for a sign.*

Paul was quoting **Isaiah 28:11**.

Isaiah 28:11 *For with stammering lips and another tongue will he speak to this people.*

This is especially pointed considering that Paul quotes Isaiah's original statement regarding another "tongue" in the plural as "tongues". This is just simple biblical use of grammar. When a foreign language is being referred to, it is a tongue, when multiple foreign languages are being referred to, they are "tongues". With this proper grammatical understanding, Isaiah's statement simply means that another "tongue" other than their own would be used. The fact is that there are many other "tongues" other than their own, and Paul made that point by referring to this in the plural.

1 Corinthians 14:26 *How is it then, brethren? when ye come together, every one of you hath a psalm, hath a doctrine, hath **a tongue**, hath a revelation, hath an interpretation. Let all things be done unto edifying.*

Even this verse, which uses "tongue" in the singular, actually further proves the point I am making. It is not that every one of you has ***the tongue*** (the only one spoken, as you seem to be inferring), but that everyone has ***a tongue***. Grammatically, that means that they potentially have different tongues they are speaking in.

BRO. V.M.: Speaking in tongues is a miraculous occurrence where an individual is moved upon by the Holy Ghost to speak in a language, absent an interpreter with that gift, only known to God. It is the fulfillment of prophecy and is a sign to the unbelieving.

BRO. BAER: Amen. I agree. Though with the caveat that languages can also be spoken that could be understood by others present if God wanted that to be the case and if they knew those languages. This is what I believe we are seeing in **Acts 2** and elsewhere and in experiences I know occurred in my day that I am neither speculating on or spiritually foolish enough to be deceived by.

The fact is that it would not matter at all if someone was speaking Tagalog when they were worshiping if no one in the building spoke that language. They would still be understood only by God. The only examples of where this privacy of communication between God and the individual might change is if He allowed them to speak in a human tongue when someone who spoke that tongue might be present for the sake of the one hearing it: to evidence that the person speaking in it, who they know does not know that language, could only be doing so by the genuine inspiration of the Spirit. I have told the story before of Bro. Moore's father and mother, and how his mother, speaking in tongues in fluent French was what convinced his father (who did not believe in speaking in tongues) of the reality of that spiritual experience. Bro. Moore's mother speaking in French accomplished exactly that. His father knew she did not know any of that language and when she spoke in it, it was evidence to him that it could only have been God who was causing her to speak in tongues in the French language, and the message to him in that language accomplished that as well… resulting in him seeking and being filled with the Holy Spirit. In order to deny these kinds of experiences you have to make many millions of people (likely including most in our body of churches) either liars or delusional… neither of which I accept.

BRO. V.M.: I disagree, tongues are definitely not a human language.

1 Corinthians 14:2 *For he that speaketh in an unknown tongue speaketh not unto men, but unto God: for **no man understandeth him**; howbeit in the spirit he speaketh mysteries.*

BRO. BAER: So, you are going to base your entire conclusion on one single verse? And, a verse that would be better understood in light of the many other verses which appear to state or imply exactly the opposite of your narrow interpretation of that verse. Once again (and I have yet to hear a single refutation from you of this point), there is no "unknown" tongue in **1 Corinthians 14**. This single example, and perhaps the parallel type of statement in **Romans 8:26**, does not change our conception of this at all. All that this single statement (taken in context) is referring to is that someone speaking to God ("unto God" and not "unto men") is having a closed conversation that isn't intended to be understood by others. Thus, "no man understandeth him". But, if God wanted the statements a person is making in tongues to be understood by others, they certainly could be (as is clearly what is occurring in **Acts 2**, etc.).

Let me point out that I am not talking about someone have a "private" personal conversation with God in tongues that is being revealed to others. I am talking about someone either testifying in a specific prophetic way to another (as in the example I gave) or someone praising God in a language that they do not know but which someone else knows and hears them using. This latter case was one of the most dramatic things that drew attention to the Pentecostal movement in the beginning of the twentieth century, and that caused several unbelievers to realize it was genuine. A person who someone knew did not know a certain language spoke in that language, exactly as described in **Acts 2**.

BRO. V.M.: Dear brother, you must read much closer, that is not what took place at all. Corinthians is rendered even more important in light of what precious little we have regarding tongues.

BRO. BAER: That is exactly what took place.

Acts 2:6-11 *Now when this was noised abroad, the multitude came together, and were confounded, because that **every man heard them speak in his own language**. And they were all amazed and marvelled, saying one to another, Behold, are not all these which speak Galilaeans? And **how hear we every man in our own tongue**, wherein we were born? Parthians, and Medes, and Elamites, and the dwellers in Mesopotamia, and in Judaea, and Cappadocia, in Pontus, and Asia, Phrygia, and Pamphylia, in Egypt, and in the parts of Libya about Cyrene, and strangers of Rome, Jews and proselytes, Cretes and Arabians, **we do hear them speak in our tongues the wonderful works of God**.*

No one reading this would conclude that they were all actually speaking one single language and all these different folks with different dialects instead just heard their own language, even though that was not actually what was being spoken. That is not what this passage is describing at all. There is no biblical basis for such an interpretation.

I agree about 1 Corinthians though, as I have pointed out in great detail already, the actual language and grammar of **1 Corinthians 14** does not support your view… in fact, just the opposite. If you can better explain the verses and commentary that I gave on them, please do so, as I see no other reasonable or rational way to understand them. We do have to pay attention to the actual language and choice of grammar the Spirit inspired. If you disagree with the commonly held understanding of those statements just go back to those verses and explain them better. Show, for example, how Paul speaking in other tongues (plural) in the exact same context that he is talking about someone speaking in another tongue (singular) means something other than what it seems to say (with any common sense reading).

BRO. E.F.: Bro. M., I've been behind the pulpit and began preaching on a thought that God brought to my mind, and it took on a life of its own coming from my heart and my understanding through my studies. I have started with that thought and stayed up for an hour or so, and it makes me believe that the Holy Ghost can speak in English, which is my native tongue, but if a Spanish speaking person was there who didn't know what I was saying it would be unknown to him. Even someone who understands English, if God doesn't open his eyes to what is being said, it will be unknown to him to. Tongues are for a sign to the unbeliever (**1 Corinthians 14:22**). Their purpose is to transform you into a believer. The Holy Ghost can move upon someone to speak all kinds of different languages or tongues.

BRO. V.M.: Brethren, you do not have not one single scripture to support tongues ever being a human language. When Peter and the disciples began to speak on Pentecost every man, no matter what his language out of the many, understood him. He could not have been speaking twenty languages at the same time. The miracle was that these people observed the crowd knowing it was made up of many different languages yet each and every one understood (heard) in their particular language the words of Peter and the disciples. That is what astounded them! They would not have been astounded simply hearing them speak another language, they didn't know what languages that Peter or the disciples spoke. I hope you will consider what I am saying, because I assure you it is the truth.

BRO. BAER: Peter was not the one they heard speaking in the dialects of the lands they came from. That event *preceded* Peter's sermon. Those hearing the different languages spoken were Jews who were part of the dispersia who heard the 120 all speaking in other tongues (**Acts 2:4**). Though they had grown up in areas with different languages and dialects they almost certainly all spoke Aramaic, which is what Peter would have been speaking, and Peter (by himself) did not start speaking to them until after they had heard the 120 speaking in various tongues (**Acts 2:14**). You are so determined that you cannot be incorrect that you cannot or will not allow yourself to see just how obvious the language of this passage is to anyone reading it.

My friend you have assured us that the views you hold on all of the things you have contradicted us on (in far more discussions than just this one, and often with the same kind of unbiblical ideas) are "the truth". The problem with that claim, as I have tried to communicate to you as gently as possible, is that it essentially communicates that you must be the repository of more truths than any or all of us put together, and that only those truths you declare are truth are actually truth... no matter how obtuse or irregular their interpretation, no matter how much evidence we give against them (which you have left entirely unrefuted), and no matter that no one but you seems to see them. The evidence against some of your very dogmatic claims (including this one) is very heavy, but you don't even seem to feel its weight, and don't even appear conscious of its presence. I'll ask again, and I mean it in love... Show a better way of interpreting the many passages we have given that contradict your view. Just give a better interpretation of the meaning of each that is more biblically consistent and linguistically accurate. All I am hoping for on this is that if you actually do so, one day you may read back through and truly consider all the evidences in an honest and objective way and realize how much more unbiblical and unreasonable your claims are.

BRO. V.M.: Of course it was Peter. Why do you make so many assertions knowing I can't possibly address all of them? Let's take one at a time shall we?

Acts 2:14 *But Peter, standing up with the eleven, lifted up his voice, and said unto them, Ye men of Judaea, and all ye that dwell at Jerusalem, be this known unto you, and hearken to my words:*

BRO. BAER: Forgive me as I did not realize I was making "many assertions". My (perhaps incorrect) impression was that I was giving several simple biblical statements and grammatical facts that are problematic for your claims. Regarding your claim that Peter was the only one who they heard speak in all their dialects (when doing so would have been absolutely unnecessary as they all would have also spoken Aramaic), that claim is so incorrect as to be befuddling. **Acts 2:4** states that they were *all* filled with the Holy Ghost and began to speak with other *tongues* (plural), not just an "unknown" tongue (the fact that there actually is no reference in the original language of the Bible to an "unknown" tongue is just one example of something you refuse to refute or accept). **Acts 2:5-13** tells us who was hearing them *all* speaking in other *tongues* and hearing their own *dialects*. That occurred *before* Peter stood up to speak individually in **Acts 2:14**. In addition, Peter referred back to what these Jews were hearing as "*these* (plural: the whole group) are not drunken". The only "these" he could be referring to is the group of those in the upper room who *had been* speaking in other *tongues* (plural). He is only one of that group and he is *never* mentioned as the only one doing the speaking in tongues. His speech does not even begin until *after* he addressed these folks who had *already* heard the whole group of the 120 (plural) speaking in other tongues. Why can you not see this my brother? No one would argue what you are arguing. It is not at all what **Acts 2** states or infers.

BRO. V.M.: Was Peter present with the 120? Was he filled with the Holy Ghost with the 120? Did he speak with tongues as did the 120? Did the people hear Peter speak in tongues? I rest my case.

BRO. BAER: Of course we believe Peter was *one of* the 120 speaking in *tongues*. I can only assume you are making these statements to avoid the actual issue. The fact that he was one of them does not make him the only one speaking one single "tongue" that all the Jews there heard. The 120 were speaking in "tongues", not a "tongue" or the "tongue", and all of them were doing so. The people heard them *all* speak in tongues, not just Peter.

BRO. V.M.: I ask you to take one subject at a time. Why then, when we are discussing tongues, do you decide to bring in a disagreement regarding Peter?

BRO. BAER: We have never left the subject of "tongues". It was your point, and not mine, that the "tongues" in **Acts 2** that the Jews were hearing were actually only one "tongue" that Peter was speaking in but that they were all individually hearing in different "tongues". Unless you are trying to avoid the inherent contradictions involved in your claim, I am surprised you would make such a statement. We are discussing "tongues" as you said. How could going to **Acts 2** to explain that they are "tongues" (plural) being spoken rather than just one "tongue" (as you believe) be changing the subject?

BRO. V.M.: Okay, let us get back to the subject. Where is tongues ever described as a known human language?

BRO. BAER: I can't see any place where we have left the subject. Is **Acts 2** and the "tongues" spoken there another subject?

The household of Cornelius in **Acts 10:46** spoke with *tongues* (plural), just as we so often see this word used: as *tongues* (plural). Given that there is no basis or rationale for claiming these *tongues* (plural) are actually just one tongue (singular), then that only leaves us with two options. These are different celestial tongues (which there is no biblical support for), or these are either celestial and terrestrial tongues, or different terrestrial tongues (both of which are biblically supported).

BRO. V.M.: Where is tongues ever described as a known human language?

BRO. BAER: The twelve men of Ephesus in **Acts 19:6** spoke with *tongues* (plural). Again, this can only refer to one of the options I just mentioned.

As to the singular or plural of a word, this is also something I have discussed in great detail already in this conversation, once again either ignored or overlooked by you. Whether it is singular "tongue" or plural "tongues" is highly significant. The whole basis of your argument is that there is only one "tongue" (singular) when the far more common use of that term is in the plural: "tongues". "Tongues" in the plural refer to more than one tongue. Unless you believe they are speaking multiple angelic tongues the only other possibility is that they are speaking the tongues of man and/or angels, which is exactly what the Bible calls them (**1 Corinthians 13:1**).

BRO. V.M.: Consider my position. Because of my belief that tongues is never a known human language all these people who have claimed they spoke in tongues as known languages and their teachers who enable them to believe such a thing must be deluded. There is no middle of the road. Sorry, but truth must be told.

BRO. BAER: Claiming this view of yours is truth is dangerously self-deceptive when you have no biblical basis for such a claim. You entire claim is constructed out of a very odd, contextually contradictory, biblically unfaithful, and grammatically impossible method of interpretation. Added to that is your highly subjective view of historical experiences that you could not possibly refute as you were not present when many of them even occurred. Are you actually considering what you are claiming? Let me ask you again, as you never answer have answered this question, are you claiming that your personal (supposed) spiritual insights and experiences trump all of the many millions of believers who claim to have had such experiences, and the many God called, Spirit-filled and Spirit-anointed ministers who teach differently from you? Why are you to be depended on as more spiritual and more knowledgeable than all others? Why would your interpretation (which breaks the rules of grammar and is in no way biblically consistent) be more viable than that of many other Spirit-filled men of God who would never come to such a conclusion?

BRO. V.M.: Brother, you can't show one scripture to refute my interpretation, but I can provide one that supports it, yet I am somehow at fault? Astounding.

1 Corinthians 14:2 *For he that speaketh in an unknown tongue speaketh not unto men, but unto God: for no man understandeth him; howbeit in the spirit he speaketh mysteries.*

BRO. BAER: Are you claiming that one passage refutes the many uses of the plural "tongues" in the Bible, which it would have to directly contradict in order to do so? Come on now. When someone speaks in *a* "tongue" it is just referring in a general way to someone speaking a language other than their own. When one single person is said to speak in "tongues" it is referring to more than one language other than their own. That is very simple grammar, and we find both uses of those terms and grammatical structures in **1 Corinthians 14**. As I have already pointed out multiple times (with no response), Paul himself said that he spoke with *tongues* (plural) and not just in a *tongue* (singular). The very chapter you keep referencing has several examples of plural *tongues* being spoken by a single individual that entirely disproves your blatant misuse of these terms and of the grammar associated with them.

BRO. V.M.: Let me be clear, the singular or plural use of the word has absolutely nothing to do with whether or not the gift of tongues (plural) includes known foreign languages. It clearly does not.

BRO. BAER: There is absolutely nothing "clear" about such a statement. I do my best to avoid highly dogmatic and confrontational statements on these kinds of issues if possible, but that is patently false my brother. If there are *tongues* (plural) then they either are different kinds of angelic tongues (which you do not believe), they are a combination of angelic tongues and human tongues, or they are different kinds of human tongues. Which is it you believe? I know you don't believe (and there is absolutely no biblical evidence or inference of such a thing) that these are different kinds of angelic tongues. Once more, in the very same book, Paul makes the following statement (just preceding the statements of **1 Corinthians 14** by the way).

1 Corinthians 13:1 *Though I* (singular) *speak with the **tongues*** (plural) ***of men and of angels*** (either or both the tongues of men and/or angels)….

In order for you to keep making the incorrect claims you do about a handful of uses of the word "tongue" in the singular in **1 Corinthians 14**, you have to continue ignoring or reinventing the use of the plural word "tongues", not only in that same chapter but elsewhere in the Bible as well. And, in the passage I just quoted, Paul is clearly referring to himself individually (one single person) being able to speak in the tongues of men (that is human language my friend) and/or of angels. There is no way to avoid these simple points without either ignoring what the Bible actually says in the language and grammar it actually says it in, or reinventing the only possible meaning of these kinds of statements with your own custom created rules of language and grammar that entirely overwrite the clear statements of the Bible.

ARI'EL INSTITUTE

HOLY SPIRIT BAPTISM AND THE HOLY PLACE

BRO. T.G.: Symbolically, where does a soul become born again or receive the baptism of the Holy Ghost, in the Holy Place or in the Holy of Holies?

BRO. BAER: As far as I know, it has been our universal teaching (in our body of churches) that when you receive the Holy Spirit you (symbolically speaking) pass through the spiritual door from the Outer Court (using the symbolism of the Tabernacle of Temple) into the spiritual Holy Place. It takes the spiritual work symbolized by the elements within the Holy Place to take you on to perfection and to allow you to pass through the veil just as Jesus passed through the veil of his flesh (**Hebrews 10:20**) and opened up the way into Holy of Holies where only absolute purity (perfection) can exist without being consumed by the fiery presence (*shekinah* glory) of the Almighty

BRO. K.S.: The Holy Place. The Holy Ghost baptism puts us in fellowship and reconciles us back to God and this arrangement takes place in the Holy Place.

BRO. A.M.: I have been taught that, but it would be interesting to see the principle laid out in the Scripture. I fear though that it would be quite lengthy because it touches on the interpretation of the (spiritual) heavens. I fear we would have to explain those to explain this and who knows where else it might lead.

BRO. BAER: It would be lengthy, as you said. One starting point might be looking at what is in the Holy Place and what it symbolically represents as related to things available to the believer after he receives the Holy Spirit. A simpler approach (which would still start with symbolic interpretation) would be to look at how the Tabernacle structure is progressive in nature. Each entry is moving closer and closer to being directly in the presence of God (within the Holy of Holies). From the gate of the courtyard (which we've generally associated with going through the "door of faith" into relationship with the Lord), past the brazen altar and laver (the blood of Christ's sacrifice and the washing of the water of the word) and then on into the Holy Place (through another entry: the door of the Tabernacle) where the lampstand (the sevenfold light or even seven spirits), the shewbread (the apostles' doctrine or just pure doctrine and order in general), and the golden altar just before the veil (where I believe the last vestiges of the carnal nature are burned away, allowing entry into the Holiest of All).

We can look at how the forward movement from outside the courtyard all the way into the Holiest occurs. If each entry is a key event in terms of progressive salvation, and the first (the gate) is clearly representing entry into a relationship with the Lord by faith, it would seem very likely (and of course there are many other reasons for this) that the next entry point (the door of the Tabernacle) into a deeper relationship would be the baptism of the Holy Spirit, and the final point of entry (the veil of the Holiest) would be the point of transition into the deepest relationship of all, represented by the process of fire baptism, overcoming, and full perfecting that results in the ability to enter into the Holiest (spiritually speaking): to be in the highest and most intimate level of relationship with the Lord that is possible.

BRO. M.M.: All very good thoughts. I'm very thankful that Jesus sacrificed himself for us and that the veil was rent in two allowing us access. What are your thoughts on Paul's experience about being called up unto third heaven? Did he stand outside and peer in, or did he actually enter?

Revelation 3:12-13 *Him that overcometh will I make a pillar in the temple of my God, and he shall go no more out: and I will write upon him the name of my God, and the name of the city of my God, which is new Jerusalem, which cometh down out of heaven from my God: and I will write upon him my new name. He that hath an ear, let him hear what the Spirit saith unto the churches.*

It will be wonderful to reach the place he has for us and never go out again.

BRO. BAER: For my part, I think it was "(un)to" and not "into". I think he was, metaphorically speaking, looking into third heaven. The veil had been opened to let him look in. The Greek word ***heos***, translated "to" in the phrase caught up "to" third heaven normally refers to getting right up to something (in time or location), though not necessarily into it or past it. That is why most of the more literal translations (including the *King James Version*) translate it "to" rather than "into". It can be translated "up to the point of". When we think of being up to the point of doing something we mean that we are right there but have not done it yet.

BRO. A.J.: I see why this question is posed. The word tells us that we have access to the Father by faith and that Jesus paved the way for us to do so. We have access to approach the throne of grace, but that throne is in third heaven (the Holiest of All). But, no man has ascended themselves into heaven, except the Son of man. Paul, with all of his revelations, was only able to get up to the second veil and not into (the Holiest). But, he was able to perceive and hear third heaven conversation. I have also had an experience with prayer that felt like I transcended the usual spirit led, tongue talking prayer, and entered into a higher level in which I could not even speak anything. There was nothing to say for the glory that I felt. There was nothing to ask for.

BRO. BAER: The "into Paradise" in the next verse is what is trickier, and leads some to believe he went ***into*** the third heaven, though, the Greek word *eis*, translated "into" in the *King James Version* can actually mean "to". If so, this could still mean "up to" and not "into".

BRO. K.S.: Paul himself confirms by saying he was in paradise and caught up to third heaven. That shows us that they are two separate places (of course being spiritual conditions). Then he says he heard things, but he never saw anything, giving evidence that he was in but only up to it. Close enough to hear what was going on.

BRO. BAER: I am not sure I'm following Bro. S. Both of the Greek words refer to the same kind of thing: essentially "up to" and "to". *Eis* in **2 Corinthians 12:4** can mean "to" or "into", and thus, does not tell us clearly which was intended. Normally though, in the kind of Greek grammar present in this passage, the first statement in **2 Corinthians 12:2** ("to the third heaven") is not being contrasted with **2 Corinthians 12:4** ("to Paradise"), but paralleled. Hebrew speakers very often use this exact type of paralleling of statements (no matter what language they are speaking in) to talk about something that is one and the same thing, which would mean that if this is following the normal and most commonly used form of this kind of grammatical and colloquial expression, Paul would be referring to the same thing as "third heaven" that is "Paradise" and the word *heos* ("up to") in **2 Corinthians 12:2** would have to be referring to the same thing *eis* ("to" or "into") is referring to in **2 Corinthians 12:4**. So, using proper grammar and recognizing this as Hebrew parallelism, third heaven would equal Paradise. His being "caught up to" it in **2 Corinthians 12:2** means the same thing in **2 Corinthians 12:4**, which would have to mean that **2 Corinthians 12:4** is more likely referring to being caught up "to" rather than caught up "into".

BRO. T.G.: Yes, I don't think the thief on the cross was in the same spiritual place that the apostle Paul himself had reached in his life through the faith in Jesus Christ. Two totally different conditions.

BRO. B.M.: With the present day understanding that we now possess, I'm a bit perplexed as to why we refer to the miraculous event of becoming a true son of God as receiving the Holy Spirit. The Holy Spirit is the catalyst that causes an individual to be born again. Being born again is an act of God, creating a spirit being that is free of sin. Jesus's reference to this was telling Nicodemus that to see the kingdom of God, he must be born again. He didn't mention receiving the Holy Spirit. Paul did when addressing some at Ephesus. But in **Acts 19:6** he explains the process.

Romans 8:7 *Because the carnal mind is enmity against God: for it is not subject to the law of God, neither indeed can be.*

So, there must be a new birth take place so that we become true sons of God.

BRO. BAER: I would generally agree. I think there is a vast difference between a "son" in the womb (who hasn't been born yet), a newborn, or even a developing son, and the final, fully matured product that is the kind of son of God that Jesus was and that the overcomers are to be.

Revelation 21:7 *He that overcometh shall inherit all things; and I will be his God, and he shall be my son.*

BRO. B.M.: Referring to your observation of the similarly between Jesus and a fully matured overcomer, would you mind commenting on what differences there would be between Jesus and those overcomers? I'm not referring to "the chain of command". Excuse my limited vocabulary.

What does it mean to "inherit all things"?

BRO. BAER: Other than in specialized areas like authority, position, knowledge, power, etc. I think the Bride will be given all things that a human being is able of inheriting. I believe this would amount to the highest level of delegated authority, power, existence, etc. other than that of Christ and, of course, God his Father.

BRO. D.D.P.: Interesting question. I'm well aware of the teaching on the symbolism of the Tabernacle, but I have often asked this question myself. From what I have witnessed over the years, when a person initially receives the Holy Ghost, they tend to dance in the spirit, or at least become so overcome by the Spirit that they are not aware of their surroundings. They are in "another world".

It was not in the Holy Place, but rather in the Holy of Holies that the priest was "overcome" and would dance in the Spirit. If we consider the Holy of Holies as God's dwelling place (third heaven), then no man could enter in. However, since the mercy seat is described as a "meeting place" between God and man, then there may be something more to the symbolism of the Holy of Holies.

Since the flesh must be killed in the outer courts, then we must dwell there, but we can still partake of the purity of the Holy Place in our thoughts and daily study. Beyond that, there are times we are overcome by the Spirit and tend to lose consciousness of the world around us.

I think it might behoove us to step back and give the symbolism of the Tabernacle further consideration.

To add to my previous thoughts, the three-level design of Noah's ark has been compared to the Tabernacle. It was not just in the upper level (Holy of Holies) that the dove ascended, but through the window in that upper level.

BRO. BAER: Bro. P., I'm not sure I'm following your reference to the priest dancing in the Spirit or being overcome in the Spirit in the Holiest. The only examples I can think of that describe priests potentially being in (or at least in the entry with the curtain opened) of the Holiest Place was on the Day of Atonement, and that was a very solemn and serious ritual. There was no dancing involved. What passages are you thinking of that might validate your belief about this? From the general perspective of the brethren, it is not our flesh which was offered up in the courtyard, but that of Christ: the sacrifice of Christ. We can't offer up ourselves as living sacrifices without being in the Spirit. Now, mind you, this is just how I have seen this, and I am interested in hearing where your connections are being made on some of these points. My conception is that we have to come to the place where we go in and go out *no more*, and that would appear to happen within the building rather than out in the courtyard. Another element is Christ going through the veil of his flesh to open up the new and living way to us, which is the way into the Holiest.

BRO. D.D.P.: Forgive me for not being more specific Bro. Baer. I am actually referencing extrabiblical sources. Jewish tradition holds that the high priest had dried pomegranates tied to his legs, and a rope that extended out of the Holy of Holies. As long as the pomegranates could be heard, they know the high priest was "alive and kicking". If there was no noise, they knew he had sin in his life and had been struck dead. They pulled the body out with the rope in that event. While I tend to take all tradition with a grain of salt, I have read about this more than once over the years, so I am assuming there is some validity to it.

As for the outer courts, Jesus was our sacrifice for sin, but we must still kill the flesh on a daily basis. Resisting temptation is a sacrifice of the flesh, so I do see us as having to dwell in a place, or condition, where we can offer our desires of the flesh as a sacrifice. I would think this would have to be in the outer courts as opposed to the outer encampment or the Holy Place.

I guess I should add that I see the encampment as symbolic of the church (God's people). Just going to church is a start, but we must individually move into the outer courts and offer ourselves as sacrifices (initial repentance).

BRO. BAER: I have heard that tradition referred to many times as well. It is quoted by a good number of folks online and even in books, and I have even heard ministers among us use it in one form or another. The actual tradition is that it was the bells and pomegranates that were heard (the one causing the other to chime). I heard a very educated scholar once say that it is essentially an urban myth that has been repeated so many times that it is assumed to be true, which caused me to go looking for its origin. When I went back to the very oldest sources I could find that mentioned anything like it, they all referenced that tradition only referring to working in the Holy Place and tied its possible origin to the actions of Nadab and Abihu, who died in the Holy Place offering strange fire. The general work of the priests was only in the Holy Place, other than one single time a year when the High Priest opened the veil between the Holy Place and Holiest to sprinkle the blood on and before the Ark on the Day of Atonement.

Hebrews 9:7 *But into the second went the high priest alone once every year, not without blood, which he offered for himself, and for the errors of the people:*

Just like what we have been discussing, the word translated "into" in the *King James Version* is the Greek word ***eis***, which can be translated "up to" or "to" as well. The point being that it was only the high priest doing this (no other priest), and it was only one time in the entire year.

On the overall structure, the most common view among us has been that the camp spiritually represents "first earth" (the present world), the courtyard represents "first heaven", the Holy Place "second heaven", and the Holiest "third heaven". All of this, of course, being the spiritual meaning of the literal locations. I understand that Israel was the people of God, but if they did not have the sacrifices made for them, etc. (the work going on in the Tabernacle as a whole) they would not be able to be in a relationship with God, which is one reason we haven't seen the camp in general as the church. They are only the church to the extent that they are in, coming into the courtyard and, at least in type, further in.

One point of the preceding structural interpretation is that the three sections of the Tabernacle (the courtyard, Holy Place, and Holiest) are symbolic of first, second, and third heaven spiritual states (conditions). Thus, there is no being in the church if you are not at least in a first heaven spiritual state. That would mean that to truly be in the church you would have to have entered into the courtyard through the gate: the door of faith.

BRO. D.D.P.: I am not in disagreement with what has been taught Bro. Baer, and the basic symbolism does apply in an "overall" or "general" application. What I see is more, or perhaps alternative, representations of the Tabernacle.

As for my view on the symbolism of the camp, there was "Israel" (the camp), and the rest of the world. I see the rest of the world as atheists, Buddhists, Hindus, etc. These "ites" are not Christian in their beliefs. Today, even Judaism is not part of the camp, and some might include false "Christian" religions as being outside the camp. The camp itself is Christianity, or Christendom. Many people can claim to be a Christian, and many people in the church can claim to be children of God, but unless a person makes the individual commitment to give their life to God (sacrifice them selves), they are nothing more than what a Jew living in the camp would have been if they did not offer their required sacrifices. Since I have met many people who I truly believe have the Holy Ghost, but have never heard of the body, I can't limit the camp, or the "church", to one exclusive group.

In my assessment, the outer courts would still be first heaven, the Holy Place would be second heaven, and the Holy of Holies would be third heaven. Where my perspective probably differs the most with the common teaching is that in this particular application, I don't see third heaven as God's dwelling place, but rather God's "meeting place" with humanity, thus the description of the mercy seat in **Exodus 25:21-22**.

Exodus 25:21-22 *And thou shalt put the mercy seat above upon the ark; and in the ark thou shalt put the testimony that I shall give thee. And there I will meet with thee, and I will commune with thee from above the mercy seat, from between the two cherubims which are upon the ark of the testimony, of all things which I will give thee in commandment unto the children of Israel.*

I am aware that the Holy of Holies is considered God's dwelling place, but to me, this sounds more like God is communicating with the high priest from above the mercy seat as opposed to God "existing" within the Holy of Holies. I think we all know that God never actually lived in the Holy of Holies any more than he lived on top of Mount Sinai.

We know the high priest only entered the Holy of Holies once a year on the Day of Atonement, as you point out. I see this as Jesus being our high priest, and his death being the blood that was sprinkled on and before the Ark. I'm pretty sure you believe this as well. However, we need to keep in mind that the Passover lamb was not the sacrifice offered on the Day of Atonement. Although it is correct to say that three times a year was the minimum that an adult male had to appear at the **Beit ha-Mikdash** (Temple) to bring **korbanot** (offerings) associated with the three festivals, there are actually five types of offerings required in scripture.

Where my view picks up at is after this. Once the veil was rent in two, we now have access to the Holy of Holies. While I won't argue this is symbolic of our ability to "go to heaven" after we die, I also see it as an ongoing opportunity for us to commune with God through Christ. Perhaps this makes Jesus our mercy seat, but that might become a tangent discussion. In any event, those who adhere to the "once saved, always saved" concept, or those who claim we must still follow the law claim that Jesus was the one and only sacrifice, so his sacrifice did away with the need for all animal sacrifice. While this is true in a sense, Jesus only died once. His death was indeed our "final sacrifice" in the sense he made it possible for us to gain eternal life, but Jesus did not die so all men would be saved, but rather so that all men could be saved. He made *his* sacrifice for us, but we must still make our own sacrifices. Like the rest of the law, our sacrifice is not literal in meaning, but spiritual, just as I explained that Jesus was not a literal lamb, but spiritually represented the Passover lamb. For those who would try to keep the law literally today, they are going to fail unless they move to Israel, the Temple is rebuilt, the Levitical priesthood is reestablished, and they make their own animal sacrifices. Of course, this literal act would be an abomination to God, but we must offer our own "flesh" as our offering. Of course, by that I mean our carnal desires, temptations of the flesh, etc.

So, before I go too far off on a tangent, I see the Tabernacle as more than just a general view of first, second, and third heaven. Just as it was the center of the Jewish world, it is the spiritual center of our world if we are going to give our life to God and serve him like we should.

As for the dried pomegranate idea, I don't know if it's legitimate or not. What I do know, and I'm sure you do as well, is that there are times people become so immersed in the spirit that they might collapse while speaking in tongues, or might dance uncontrollably. I'm not talking about the typical expression of joy we often see when people are down front dancing around, but the somewhat rare (these days) times when someone is so overcome with the spirit that they are completely oblivious to the world around them. You could probably slap them upside the head and it wouldn't bring them out of it. You know, those times we so long for. I would have to imagine that since the high priest was in the "presence of God", at least spiritually, he had to have a similar experience inside the Holy of Holies.

I guess I don't see third heaven so much as God's dwelling place, but like first and second heaven, it was a condition created out of necessity so God could deal with humanity after Adam and Eve's fall. Once there is a new heaven and new earth, then just as there will be no more need for a first and second heaven condition, I don't think there will be a need for a third heaven condition, as God himself will dwell with us according to scripture.

BRO. BAER: I would agree with a number of your points. One of the principal differences might be some feathered edges on the issues of the spiritual states that are symbolized by the three heavens. Though I am not averse to the idea of the high priest going all the way into the Holiest, the biblical (and even historical) record only describes him as opening the veil (and only on the day of Atonement) and standing close enough (in the "doorway" or only just inside) to sprinkle the blood upon and before the Ark. Given the close proximity of the Ark to the veil, there would be no need to even step inside to sprinkle the blood, and certainly no need to step fully inside to do so. The Holiest was not a large room (15 feet by 15 feet at most) and the Ark was likely centered in it meaning that it would have been less than seven feet from the veil. The words the Bible uses for the high priest going "into" the Holiest can carry the meaning (and often do) of opening something up for "entry" (what the word "into" refers to is an "entry") *without* walking around inside. Given the closeness of the Ark, the high priest would have no reason to enter all the way into the Holiest as the only thing he was told to do was sprinkle the blood multiple times and then to leave. Even if he went into the Holiest fully (all the way inside rather than just standing in the doorway so to speak), it would have only been just far enough and for just long enough to sprinkle the blood and exit.

The point being that the Holiest was not a place for the kind of work that the priests did in the Holy Place. It was a very sacred space only intended to be opened just for the sprinkling of the blood and for that, only once a year. The actual, normal work going on within the Tabernacle "building" was in the Holy Place and not the Holiest.

On your points about God and the Holiest, I agree that God Himself didn't have to be fully personally present in the Holiest, but His presence through His Spirit, and even more likely through His angel (which I believe was Christ) was very much present above the Ark (from "between the cherubim").

BRO. D.D.P.: Yes, my friend, there should be no doubt that any personification of God was Jesus, and since God and Jesus are of the same spirit, then even the Spirit of God is the spirit of Jesus.

I am curious about the idea of the high priest not entering the Holy of Holies Bro. Baer. When referring to the high priest as being symbolic of Jesus, wouldn't the high priest have to have completely entered the Holy of Holies to represent Jesus ascending to the father?

By the way, I would love to discuss the "feathered edges" as time would allow. This is a topic I have been focused on for a few years now, but it is so massive that it is difficult to discuss everything in detail. I would love to hear your thoughts, contrary or otherwise, compared to the general ideas I have put forth.

BRO. BAER: I don't have any problem with the idea of the human high priests fully entering the Holiest, my main point was that the language describing them doing so can also be used to mean that they were "in" the doorway or just inside the Holiest, and *not* moving around, or ever describing as worshipping in some physical way (like dancing) within that place. They only opened the veil or entered for the purpose of getting just close enough to sprinkle the blood on and before the Mercy Seat. I do believe Christ himself is the Mercy Seat, at least in a generally symbolically sense, which is what **Romans 3:25** calls him. "Propitation" in that verse is actually the word *hilasterion*, which is the word for the "Mercy Seat", and not the word that means "propitiation" (*hilasmos*) used in **1 John 2:2** and **4:10**. The only other time that Greek word *hilasterion* is used in the Bible is in **Hebrews 9:5** where it is undoubtedly the "Mercy Seat".

The point is that the types and shadows of Christ fulfilling the role of both the high priest *and* the Mercy Seat seem to imply a greater depth and complexity in our interpretation of those elements than just the high priest opening the veil and sprinkling the blood. The main thing that I wanted to address was simply that *if* the human high priest did fully enter the Holiest (and not just stand in the entry, which the word "into" can mean) then he would not be walking around inside or doing any activity or work other than just getting close enough to sprinkle the Mercy Seat and then exiting. Given the standard stride length of a man (about 30"), even if he did enter, taking just one step forward would have put him very close to the Ark (almost within reach / touching range, if not closer), and any excess moving around could have touched or even jostled the Ark. The idea of someone "dancing around" or doing any other physically expressive actions of that kind within the Holiest Place, especially when they could easily jostle or move the Ark by doing so, is beyond what I think is reasonable to conclude.

Christ's fulfilling of these pictures is much more complex and involved than what the human high priests were doing. None of the human high priests went into the Holiest and ended up being set down (enthroned) at the right hand of God. What Christ did certainly was typified by the human high priest's work, but only in a very limited sense. The human high priest would have been terrified (or at the very least extremely careful) about opening the veil and would have gotten no closer to the Ark than absolutely necessary. The human high priests only opened that veil on the Day of Atonement, the most solemn and serious of all the feast days and would not have been moving around within the Holiest and, in my humble opinion, certainly not leaping or dancing. There was no space to do so, and the occasion of what they were doing was far too serious and solemn to have been doing so. Now, what Christ did eclipsed their actions and fulfilled their only temporal measure. What he did was different on a number of levels from the human high priests who were not opening that veil to enter into that place as a habitation (typologically, a state of spiritual existence), but were only doing a fairly quick work and closing the veil again and then exiting the Holy Place.

BRO. D.D.P.: Yes, I can see how there would be limitations when comparing the actions of the high priest to Jesus.

BRO. BAER: It is very interesting regardless, and there is a much still to be potentially discussed... so feather out some edges my brother.

BRO. D.D.P.: Well, let's start with the outer court. Do you feel it represents our initial repentance, and/or our ongoing need to sacrifice the flesh? If so, do you feel this condition did or did not exist prior to Adam sinning? If it is not initial repentance, and/or on ongoing sacrificing of our flesh, what do you see as the symbolism of "1st heaven"?

BRO. BAER: Spiritually speaking, and in its typological fulfillment, I see the outer court (first heaven condition) primarily as referring to a state of spiritual relationship with God by faith (prior to being filled with the Spirit). The court is entered by (through) faith. Under the Old Covenant, it could be spiritually "entered" by faith in God, and that relationship could be spiritually "maintained" by the blood of the sacrifices and a knowledge of and application of the word of God to their lives (the Old Covenant spiritual meaning of washing at the laver: the "washing of water by the word" (**Ephesians 5:26**). But, under the Old Covenant, Holy Spirit baptism was not available. We have seen the outer court as (at least in the Old Covenant sense) representing the period or dispensation when the highest level of relationship with God was based on faith and his word (without the full power of His Spirit yet having been given). One support for that is the dimensions of the curtains that marked off the perimeter of the courtyard (in one calculation) being about 1500 cubits, which would parallel perfectly with the 1500 years the Israelites were under the law of Moses prior to the New Covenant and the outpouring of the Holy Spirit. So, I see the courtyard (first heaven condition) as symbolically representing the place of relationship with God by faith in Him (and later in Christ as well), by the blood of sacrifices (later by the blood of Christ as *the* sacrifice), and bu the washing of the water by the word.

As to our offering up ourselves as "living sacrifices", I see that primarily occurring in the Holy Place, paralleled by the offering up of the incense at the golden altar. Though it would take a lot of detail to discuss, I'll give just a couple of the reasons why I believe this. The outer court was a place of physical sacrifices (not spiritual), whether under the Old Covenant (physical animals) *or* under the New Covenant (the physical sacrifice of Christ: his physical death for sin). We don't have to physically die as a sacrifice to completely offer up ourselves as "living sacrifices" (the very language proves that). I believe that we do so by dying out to sin, which can only occur with the empowerment of the Holy Spirit and by remaining *in* the Spirit: *in* the Holy Place. Until we come to the place where we go *in* and come *out* no more, we are in a changing state of sometimes being in the Spirit and sometimes going back out into the courtyard.

I believe some of the very things present in the courtyard are present or added to in a greater sense within the Holy Place. The brazen altar compared and contrasted with the golden altar. The washing of the water by the word at the laver compared and contrasted with the eating of the pure shewbread on the table of shewbread. What is not paralleled in the courtyard is significant as well. The sevenfold light or even seven spirits typified by the golden lampstand have no parallel in the courtyard. This does seem to represent the fact that there are things that are only truly available when in and under the full covering of the Spirit of God, which is not in the courtyard, but in the Holy Place.

BRO. T.G.: Bro. Baer, understanding what William Seymour believed in was good but had some inaccuracies, as far as their belief in the three phases of the grace of God in our salvation in Christ: justification (outer courts), sanctification (the Holy Place) and Holy Spirit baptism (the Holy of Holies).

As I understood our teachings in the Body of Christ (and how I believe) the receiving of the Holy Spirit is in the Holy Place. Our preparation is at the laver before that first veil entering into the Holy Place. I really appreciate the reading of Seymour's teachings because they really emphasized the need to sanctify and clean up their lives to prepare a soul to receive the baptism of the Holy Spirit in that waiting and that tarrying was such a significant part of us, making another step closer to God. I feel we don't emphasize that enough today, especially towards new people coming into the church: how crucial it is for a soul the Lord is dealing with who had a great conversion experience to then clean up their lives at that laver in order to receive the Holy Ghost.

We also must know the importance of the power on high in order to eat the pure shewbread and in order to receive from the seven spirits of God represented by the golden lampstand in the Holy place… in order to present ourselves perfect through Jesus Christ.

I'm seeing how important it is to go over not only the high calling in Christ Jesus that includes the message of overcoming and perfection, but new people coming into the church need the basic principles of Jesus Christ so that their faith will be made complete in him in each level of their salvation (**1 Corinthians 1:10**).

BRO. BAER: Amen. Well said. I think we can sometimes miss the power of each stage of development if we are focused on one above the others. I have seen folks get so fixated on getting people filled with the Holy Spirit (and we certainly should be heavily focused on it) that they sometimes may be get the cart ahead of the horse by trying to pray folks through to the Spirit who may have never even had a true conversion experience yet. I put a heavy emphasis not only on all the phases and stages of the process, but on all of them being absolutely genuine as well. We just had one of the folks here have a very powerful initial conversion experience that was as dramatic as any baptism in the Holy Spirit I have seen.

BRO. T.G.: Amen! Amen! Amen! I think some of this has to do with being in the Lord for many years. We expect a new soul to be converted, receive the Holy Ghost, and reach perfection in one week rather than the true process of allowing the Holy Spirit to lead that soul into higher and deeper depths in the word of God and to create a hunger and thirst after righteousness in them. We almost forget our beginning or our first experiences in the Lord. This subject needs to be shouted from the housetop. A person's conversion experience is just as important as receiving the baptism of the Holy Ghost with the evidence of speaking in tongues.

BRO. D.D.P.: That kind of touches on the next "feathered edge" my friend. The Holy Place is lined with gold, so it seems clear it represents purity and value (spiritual value as opposed to monetary value). Thus, the literal representing the spiritual. I agree that the shewbread would be the undefiled word of God (pure understanding), again the literal representing the spiritual. On the lampstands, I have heard some say it is the seven spirits of God, and some say it is God, Jesus, and the fivefold ministry. Most people seem to agree the oil is the spirit.

In the courtyard, sacrifices were indeed literal, as you mention, but you also mention we move in and out of the Holy Place. While we are in the courtyard (dealing with life in general on a daily basis), we still have the Holy Ghost. While there are times we need to "move closer" to the Lord as we face temptations, why wouldn't the literal sacrifices also have a spiritual symbolism of us killing the flesh since it is when we are "outside" and living life in general that we are faced with the temptations? I guess one way to try and restate this is if we are "in the spirit" while inside the Holy Place, when are we tempted while in that condition?

BRO. BAER: I would agree with nearly everything you are saying. We do have the Holy Spirit even when we go back out into the courtyard, but that does not necessarily mean that we are *in* the Spirit: truly living *in* and walking *in* the Spirit in the courtyard. I know many, and I know you do as well, who have received the Spirit but are seldom truly living and walking in it.

As to killing the flesh (killing our "beast"), I think (and I imagine you agree) that is principally an internal and not external thing. It means almost nothing to force external obedience if you hate what you are being forced to do, are resistant within to it, etc. We must die to the old within that motivates external sin, not merely constrain the externals. That is right at the heart of why I am spending so much time in the other ongoing discussion we have been having among the brethren on the external ritual keeping of the law of Moses. Doing so is at best only constraining external obedience and not fulfilling the far greater internal and spiritual meaning of those only external, ritual ordinances. At the worst it is empty (vain) exercise disguised as acts of productive obedience (that changes nothing within the heart).

BRO. D.D.P.: Actually, I think this topic is related to the Hebraic movement, and addresses some of the errors in their thinking Bro. Baer. Unfortunately, it is an exhaustive topic, so it isn't easy to just jump to certain points without first building a foundation.

Let's move forward a moment. When we are talking with the Lord, where are we in relation to the Tabernacle? I don't mean people going to the front of the church and speaking in tongues, but just throughout the day when we have the time to just sit and carry on a conversation with Jesus, or when he is explaining scripture to us?

I will say I do realize there are times we are talking with the Lord and think we are just speaking English (or whatever language someone speaks), and it's only when we happen to hear ourselves that we realize we are speaking in tongues. But, we are still aware of life going on around us, and we are still focusing on the events taking place that we need to, such as not driving off into a ditch. Are we in the Holy Place at that time?

BRO. BAER: I hope none of those listening to us will run off and build a doctrine on this or on the opposite side, critique this only practical point I am about to make, but, it may be that those in a situation like you are describing are living very close to the door of the Tabernacle, or even in the doorway. I mean the door into the Tabernacle proper (the three entry points are most commonly referred to as the gate of the courtyard, the door of the Tabernacle, and the veil of the Holiest).

BRO. D.D.P.: Unfortunately, there aren't too many times I get the opportunity to just "let go" and get caught up in the Spirit to the point that I become oblivious to my surroundings. When those rare occasions do present themselves, am I still living close to the door, or is that when I pass through the door temporarily?

I ask because I am trying to associate the shewbread and the candlesticks with that experience. I would think that if the shewbread represents a true understanding of the word of God, that would be something we would partake of while we are aware of our surroundings and are able to study the scriptures.

BRO. BAER: Again, I mean this practically and spiritually, I would like to think that those of us who love the Lord and hunger for a deeper relationship with Him are at least living their lives "up against" the door, if not yet perpetually in the Holy Place. When we are spiritually *in* the Holy Place, I would imagine we are seeking (again, I mean this spiritually) to live up against the veil between the Holy Place and Holiest… until we are able to pass through that veil. If we are doing the former (living within and, if without, living "close to the door"), I would imagine we would be regularly having those types of experiences in the Spirit. I believe the same about shewbread. I see it as representing the pure truth of the word of God in general, or perhaps the apostles' doctrine (given that there are twelve loaves) more particularly. But, I think we need the light of the lampstand to truly and fully see what we are eating, and to properly approach the golden altar as well.

BRO. D.D.P.: If the conditions I described earlier put us at the entrance to the Holy Place, but not in it, I am curious how you see us partaking of the word of God (the shewbread) if we are not in a condition within the Holy Place where we are not simply shouting and dancing in the spirit?

BRO. BAER: I'm not sure I follow the last. Why would we need to be shouting and dancing in the Spirit? Being in the Spirit shouldn't necessarily require someone to be shouting and dancing. They might be if that is how they are responding to the Spirit, but there are far deeper measures of being in the Spirit than just external expressions of emotion (as I know you know, so forgive me).

BRO. W.M.: There is more to the Spirit than dancing and shouting, for you need not shout nor dance to be in the Spirit.

BRO. BAER: Amen. That is very true, and we may entirely miss that fact if we pigeonhole the moving of the Spirit into only being present when we see external emotional or physical expressions going on.

BRO. D.D.P.: Perhaps I have misunderstood your previous comments Bro. Baer. If being in the Spirit to the point of talking to the Lord in tongues and not even realizing it until you hear yourself is living at the edge of the entrance to the Holy Place, then I would assume entering the Holy Place would have to be more than that. About the only thing I know that is more powerful is being so overcome with the Spirit that you are typically dancing and shouting. If not, I would imagine a person is at least so overcome by the spirit that they would not be just walking or driving around fully coherent of their surroundings.

Perhaps it would help if you could explain what you feel a person's condition is, both spiritually and consciously while in a condition of being in the Holy Place?

BRO. BAER: I think we both may be talking past each other (in the sense that we both have misunderstood each other). I believe being in the Spirit is being under its ongoing covering, under its influence and direction, etc. (which certainly wouldn't require a person be speaking in tongues and shouting all the time). As we have always believed (among our churches) tongues is an expression and witness that someone has received the Holy Spirit, but someone does not always have to talk in tongues every time they feel the Spirit, for the Spirit to inspire their thoughts, change their disposition, direct their steps, etc. Someone living and walking in the Spirit (which as we have taught it is pictured by being in the Holy Place) simply means those things (and more). It may take a dramatic manifestation of audible and other witnesses to validate that someone is "going through" or has "gone through the door", but that is not a constant activity of someone who is living and walking in the Spirit. It is just a manifestation of someone experiencing the baptism of the Spirit (passing through the door) or worshiping or praying in the Spirit.

BRO. D.D.P.: So is being in that condition necessary for understanding scripture Bro. Baer? I ask because the shewbread is in the Holy Place, so if the shewbread represents the word of God, and the candlesticks represent illumination or enlightenment, then it seems to stand to reason that the only time we could truly study the word of God would be when we are in a second heaven condition: inside of the Holy Place.

BRO. BAER: Not in a general sense, but I do think being "in the Spirit" (having the Spirit within and being inspired by it and taught by it) is necessary for some deeper truths, higher vision, etc. Someone can understand biblical truths without having been baptized in the Spirit, and prior to Christ sending it to "lead into all truth". The "all truth" that I believe is pictured by the shewbread under the illuminating light of the golden lampstand is what you will need to be in the Spirit to receive. That is why we have believed the word of God is available in the courtyard (in part as one of the pictures within the symbolism of the laver: the washing of water by the word) *and* in the Holy Place. The major difference would be a different measure or type of truth that is available within that is not available to that degree or at level of clarity without.

MATERIALS FOR FURTHER STUDY

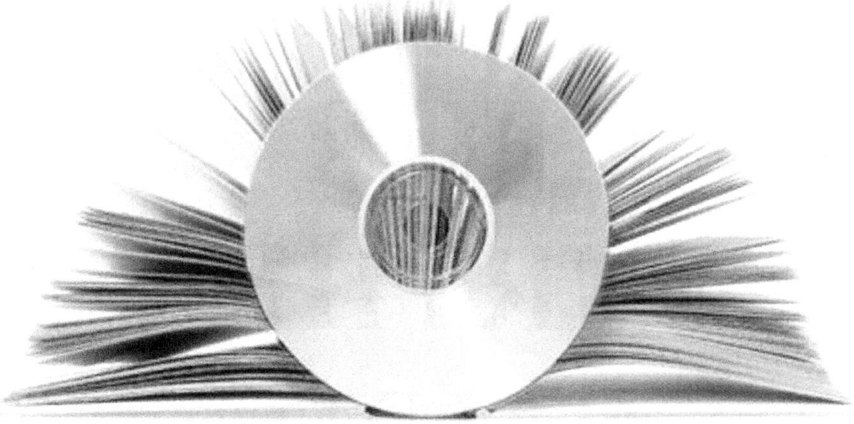

Updated and Expanded 14th ANNIVERSARY EDITION

The Incorruptible Seed will restore your faith in the Bible, as well as revealing its intricate structural design and history.

Inside you will discover:
- Undeniable evidences that verify the Bible is God's word
- Key elements that separate the Bible from every other sacred book
- Prophecies that have been indisputably historically fulfilled
- The influence of the Bible on science, medicine, literature, music, education, government, and the moral standards of western civilization
- The incredible indestructibility of the Bible
- Five methods of the Bible's inspiration
- Language and hidden design of the Bible
- The unbelievable precision of the Jewish copying of the Old Testament
- How the books of the Bible were chosen
- Definitive witnesses that determine whether a writing is part of Scripture
- The falling away of the Church and the effect this had on the Bible
- The persecution of Bible believers and attempts to keep the Bible from God's people
- History of the English translations of the Bible
- The real truth about textual criticism and its efforts to undermine faith in the Bible
- The King James Bible versus modern translations
- Hidden omissions and additions revealed in later translations of the Bible and where they originated
- And much more!

400 PAGES

Updated and Expanded 12th ANNIVERSARY EDITION
An historical, cultural, symbolic, and prophetic study
260 PAGES

Updated and Expanded 7th ANNIVERSARY EDITION
A study of the symbolism and prophetic pictures hidden within the imagery and structure of the Tabernacle of the Lord
392 PAGES

ARI'EL INSTITUTE

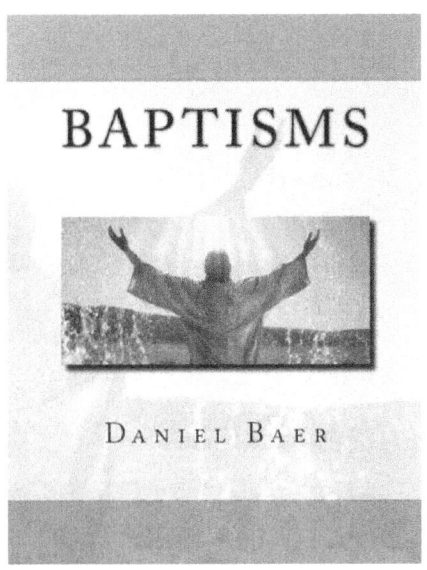

BAPTISMS — Daniel Baer

170+ pages of Bible study notes in outline form and 180+ pages of notes transcribed from live ministerial discussions, as well as five review tests and answer keys
422 PAGES

HELL EXPLAINED — Don Kosa

A study of the Doctrine of Hell from a biblical perspective (written by Bro. Don Kosa)
124 PAGES
$17.95

ARI'EL INSTITUTE

ONE GOD AND ONE LORD
PART 1
A BIBLICAL STUDY OF THE DOCTRINE OF THE GODHEAD
DANIEL BAER

Biblical, contextual, comparative, and linguistic analysis, including answers to the arguments of differing views on the Godhead, arguments against common conceptions on the Godhead, essays, tables, and much more
658 PAGES

ONE GOD AND ONE LORD
PART 2
DISCUSSIONS ON THE DOCTRINE OF THE GODHEAD
DANIEL BAER

Transcribed discussions and debate on the Godhead
654 PAGES

ARI'EL INSTITUTE

Images, illustrations, tables, and outlines of biblical subjects, including those on Types and Shadows, Prophecy and Eschatology, Biblical History, Church History, Christology, the Soul, Hell, the Resurrections, the Ministry, and many more
414 PAGES

BIBLICAL BLUEPRINTS Part 2
COMING SOON

A biblical and allegorical study of the message of restoration and redemption in the Book of Ruth
280 PAGES

ARI'EL INSTITUTE

A beginning course book on the fundamentals of reading Biblical Hebrew. Included are tests, charts, and illustrations to aid in learning the Hebrew letters, vowel points, and vocabulary
206 pages

A verse by verse commentary study of the symbolism of the Bride of Christ in the Song of Solomon (part 1)
320 PAGES

SONG OF SONGS Part 2
COMING SOON

ARI'EL INSTITUTE

A study of the beliefs regarding the identities of the individuals resurrected in Matthew 27:52: primarily being a refutation of the view that these were the Old Testament period patriarchs and prophets
**112-page book
and 3 audio CD set**

**SHADOWS AND LIGHT:
THE OLD VERSUS THE NEW COVENANT**
COMING SOON

**FRUIT OF THE SPIRIT
STUDY GUIDE**
COMING SOON

**PDF (DIGITAL) EDITIONS
OF ALL BOOKS (IN FULL COLOR)
ARE AVAILABLE**

ARI'EL INSTITUTE BIBLICAL STUDIES JOURNALS

Quarterly biblical studies journal, including Bible studies, articles, and a transcript of ministerial discussion (questions and answers) taken from the Ari'el Institute Group
(each journal is approximately 160 pages)

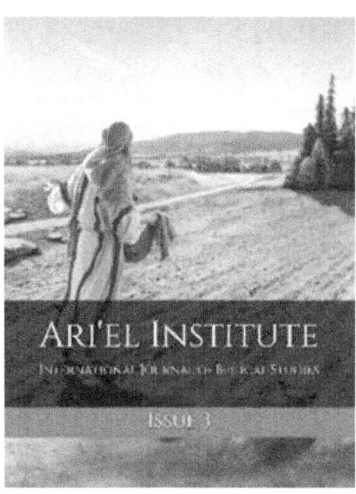

ARI'EL INSTITUTE
ISSUE 5

ARI'EL INSTITUTE
ISSUE 6

ARI'EL INSTITUTE
INTERNATIONAL JOURNAL OF BIBLICAL STUDIES
ISSUE 7

ARI'EL INSTITUTE
ISSUE 8

ARI'EL INSTITUTE
ISSUE 9

ARI'EL INSTITUTE

**PDF (DIGITAL) EDITIONS OF ALL ARI'EL INSTITUTE JOURNALS
ARE AVAILABLE**

PDF editions are digital copies of each of the journals which are able to be opened
and read on any computer, tablet, or smartphone

**PDF (DIGITAL) ANNUAL SUBSCRIPTIONS TO THE ARI'EL
INSTITUTE JOURNAL
ARE AVAILABLE**

PDF editions are digital copies of each of the journals which are able to be opened
and read on any computer, tablet, or smartphone

PDF (digital) subscriptions are emailed when each new issue becomes available
quarterly
(January, April, July, October)
New subscriptions begin with the newest issue and include four total issues.

ARI'EL INSTITUTE

CD SETS

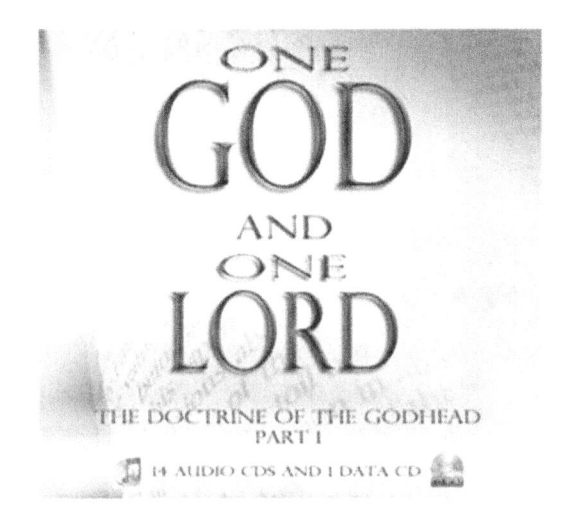

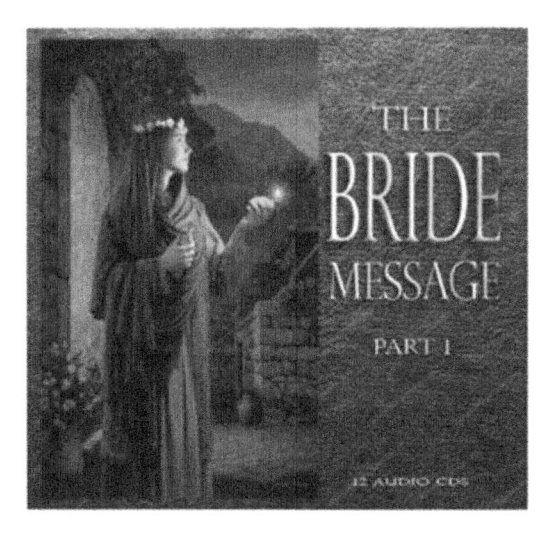

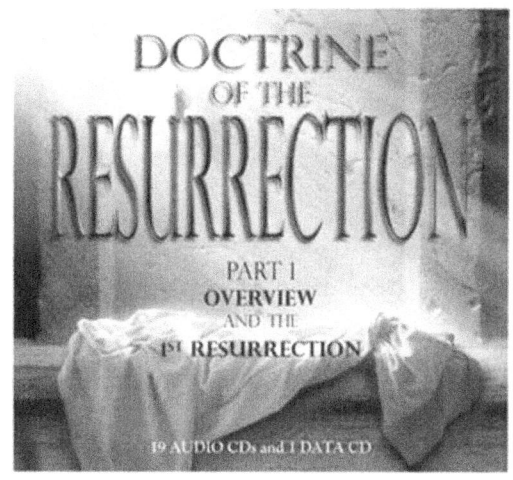

ARI'EL INSTITUTE

TABERNACLE OF THE LORD
13 AUDIO CDs and 1 DATA CD
UPDATED AND EXPANDED EDITION

THE FEASTS OF ISRAEL
UPDATED AND EXPANDED 2017 SERIES
14 AUDIO CDs

RUTH
The Message of Restoration and Redemption in the Book of Ruth
22 AUDIO CDs

THE SONG OF SONGS
The Bride of Christ in the Song of Solomon
Part 1
24 CD SET
FULL AUDIO SESSIONS ON CHAPTERS 1 - 4
(MATERIAL COVERED IN THE BOOK WITH FURTHER DISCUSSION)

ELIJAH THE PROPHET
Part 1: I Kings 17-18
8 AUDIO CDs

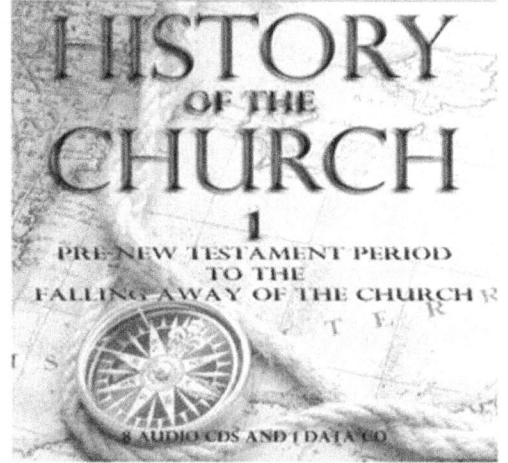

HISTORY OF THE CHURCH 1
PRE-NEW TESTAMENT PERIOD TO THE FALLING AWAY OF THE CHURCH
8 AUDIO CDS AND 1 DATA CD

ARI'EL INSTITUTE

DOCTRINE of the DEVIL
SURVEY and STUDY of the PERSON and POWER of SATAN versus the PERSONIFICATION of SATAN
15 AUDIO CDs and 1 DATA CD

HELL
THE CONSUMING FIRE AND ETERNAL JUDGMENT OF GOD
14 AUDIO CDs and 1 DATA CD

THE SABBATH
THE PHYSICAL AND SPIRITUAL 7th DAY
7 AUDIO CDs

REVELATION
PART 2
REVELATION 4:1 – 8:1
10 AUDIO CDs and 1 DATA CD

THE 12 FRUIT OF THE SPIRIT
INTRODUCTION AND THE FRUIT OF LOVE

THE 12 FRUIT OF THE SPIRIT
JOY AND PEACE

{ 153 }

SEVEN LETTERS TO THE SEVEN CHURCHES
Part 1
EPHESUS, SMYRNA, AND PERGAMOS

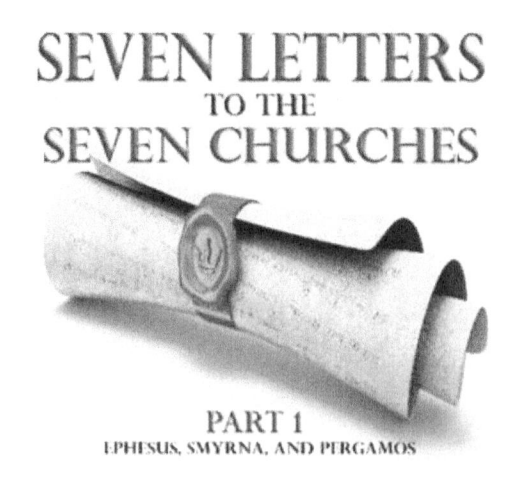

SEVEN LETTERS TO THE SEVEN CHURCHES
Part 2: Thyatira, Sardis, Philadelphia, and Laodicea
COMING SOON

FRUIT OF THE SPIRIT:
LONGSUFFERING, GENTLENESS, AND GOODNESS
COMING SOON
(FOLLOWED BY AUDIO OF CLASSES
ON THE REMAINING FRUIT OF THE SPIRIT)

ONE GOD AND ONE LORD Part 2
Advanced Issues and Apologetics
COMING SOON

SONG OF SONGS Part 2: Song of Solomon 4 – 8
COMING SOON

THE PSALMS Part 1
COMING SOON

ARI'EL INSTITUTE

MULTIMEDIA

10 YEAR ANNIVERSARY MULTIMEDIA COLLECTION
MP3 audio files, books and charts on a 32 GB FLASH DRIVE
100+ Sermons from 2005 to 2015
All topical Bible Study subjects taught from 2005 to 2015
More than 30 Ministerial Bible study sessions with visiting ministers
PDF files of all books produced from 2005 through 2015
Charts and handouts from Bible study classes

2016 ANNUAL MULTIMEDIA COLLECTION
MP3 audio files of Sermons, Bible Studies, and Ministerial Sessions,
as well as PDF files of charts, and all books published in 2016
on an 8 GB USB thumb drive

2017 ANNUAL MULTIMEDIA COLLECTION
MP3 audio files of Sermons, Bible Studies, and Ministerial Sessions,
as well as PDF files of charts, and all books published in 2017
on a 16 GB USB thumb drive

2018 ANNUAL MULTIMEDIA COLLECTION
MP3 audio files of Sermons, Bible Studies, and Ministerial Sessions,
as well as PDF files of all books published in 2018
on a 16 GB USB thumb drive

2019 ANNUAL MULTIMEDIA COLLECTION
MP3 audio files of Sermons, Bible Studies, and Ministerial Sessions,
as well as PDF files of all books published in 2019
on a 16 GB USB thumb drive

ARI'EL INSTITUTE

For information or to attend a local service or Bible study, you may contact us at

GOSPEL ASSEMBLY CHURCH
1100 S. Trimble Rd.
Mansfield, Ohio 44906
mansfieldgac@yahoo.com

Information, multimedia files, and other materials may also be found on the church website at
www.mansfieldgac.com
or at
www.facebook.com/MansfieldGAC/

Made in the USA
Columbia, SC
08 May 2020